D0892098

WHO
YOU ARE

IS HOW YOU
LEAD

RACHEL L. RIDER

Printed in the United States of America

Hardcover ISBN: 978-1-958714-71-3
Paperback ISBN: 978-1-958714-72-0
Ebook ISBN: 978-1-958714-73-7
Library of Congress Control Number: 2022950633

MUSE
LITERARY

CHICAGO-NEWYORK-PARIS-ROME

Muse Literary
3319 N. Cicero Avenue
Chicago IL 60641-9998

Contents

Acknowledgments

At the end of one of the many days that I was working on this book, I sat down to dinner with my husband.

"I just finished chapters one and two of the book," I mentioned proudly. My husband just stared at me.

"You have an infant, a three-year-old, you're managing two construction projects, a move, and running a business. How did you write chapters one and two?!" he asked in disbelief.

"Because I have a team," I replied simply.

His first reaction was, "Oh, so you didn't write the book."

It was funny and frustrating all at the same time. "I absolutely did. Every idea is mine."

"I oversaw every word," I explained. "And I did not write this alone."

I was able to walk my talk, and operate solely in my zone of genius and outsource everything else (inherent to the MettaWorks approach), because of these sacred guides and partners. I want to acknowledge that it took the light of everyone on this page to co-create this book.

The writing of this book has been a gift to me, allowing me to work on my own inner demons. Many people helped me look at myself, and become the person able to bring this book to the world. This book exists because of the teachers who helped me find myself, my voice, and my beliefs, and because of the practitioners who supported the energy required to create it.

I am deeply grateful for every person listed on this page, and any not listed who supported and believed in this book:

Jeffrey Shugen Arnold Roshi, for helping me to see beyond my thoughts to trust in my true nature. Your unconditional love, through all the storms of my life, has been a mirror, allowing me to know my true mind.

Dorothy Pietracatella, my "witch," for helping me see the experiences of my body as a gift instead of a curse, build capacity to stay in sensation, and ride the waves of discomfort, mining them for power and wisdom. Through you, I have found profound peace within the human experience, connect more deeply with people, and read the room in a way I couldn't articulate or be in charge of before.

Tami Hinden, for taking me on journeys I never thought were possible. As a healer, craniosacral therapist, and acupuncturist, you saved me from PPD. You connected me to spirit and the crystal kingdom. You taught me that physical and spiritual form can be in union. You have helped me cultivate my voice in a deeper way, and embrace and lean into my spiritual world.

Caitlin McCoskey, for your loving friendship and introduction to the power within me I never knew existed. With your guidance, I've awakened to my own ability to see energy, and learned to trust its fluidity, information, and a way to clear and clean the cobwebs of internal blockages. Your unconditional love has supported me throughout.

Joanna Lindenbaum, for being my first example of running a business as a reflection of self, integrating the spiritual and somatic, and translating that integration into success. You've helped me cultivate my relationship to my business in a much deeper way.

Charisse Sisou, for collaborating with me as an intuitive copywriter and sacred spaceholder. You listened and reflected back, and stuck with me to iterate (and iterate) until we got it right. You channeled the essence of me.

Makeda Pennycooke, my anti-racism coach, for shining a light on the cultural conditioning I was brought up in. As a constant example of compassionate accountability, you've refused to engage in the shame and held me accountable to the work. You allow me to consider the possibility of a life without so many cultural restraints.

Adriene Ingalls, for bringing your energetic intuitive power to body work, staying in it with me, and helping me find my inner and physical strength.

Fabienne Fredrickson, for showing me that a business can be wildly successful in a way that is kind and honoring of what is important to me, and for creating a community where I could be supported.

My superstar team, for allowing me to step away from the day-to-day to write the book while remaining CEO of a successful company. It is because of you that there is a book to read at all!

My mother, Susan Wilder, for introducing me to almost every important person on this list, and for always acknowledging and honoring the inner world. You endlessly have my best interests in heart and mind and it is because of you that I have made it this far, and that I do what I do.

My father, Stephen Wilder, for being my first and best editor. For bringing patience and curiosity to all my writings, with the most love. Your love is woven into the fibers of this work and book.

My brother, Nolan Wilder, for showing me that life doesn't need to be lived just one way. You were my first example of a life that doesn't need to be played by certain rules (and that's a good thing).

My children, for being my sacred mirror; when all else fails, you are the one motivator to get me to look at my stuff. You have introduced me to a new level of intimacy and love.

My husband Zac, for being my best supporter and friend. You have faith in me when I don't. You never question my wildest goals. You are steadfast in the face of the biggest difficulties. You never falter. You are my rock, and continue to evolve with me.

This book is a tapestry: the power of the people who helped create it woven in the words, the teachings and the energy itself. Each one of my teachers and relationships has been responsible for profoundly changing my life and my experience of the world around me. These teachers have generously shared their knowledge with me. Now, through this book, you too get to be a recipient of their wisdom and love.

Finally, I would like to acknowledge you, dear reader, for choosing this book. Some part of your inner world has already guided you here.

As you take this journey, I invite you to recognize your own team of support. I invite you to acknowledge who has brought you this far, who has helped you be in a position to open these pages. Who will help you get to where you want to be?

May this book be of service to you, as all of these people have been of service to me.

CHAPTER 1

The Challenge Every Leader Faces (That No One Tells You About)

*"Mastering others is strength;
mastering oneself is true power."*
—Lao Tsu

"I can't get it all done." Stephanie threw her arms up in a gesture of defeat.

"There's too much to do! I have to put together data for the board, triage several recent escalations, make sure our clients are feeling supported..." Stephanie listed all that was on her plate as an ascending VP of Customer Success. Her soft voice rising in pitch with each item, I could feel *her* panic in *my* chest. I could tell how insurmountable and overwhelming it all felt for her.

Over years of working with hundreds of executives, I've seen many hit this specific upper limit to what they can do. When leaders hit this wall, it is a really good sign. It tells me that they are truly ready to pivot. This moment is a turning point to celebrate. I want to jump up and down with them and yell, "You are right! You can't get it all done!" That is not your role at this level. Woohoo!

Though it may not seem that way as you rise through the ranks, executing and getting things done are actually the easy part. Being a successful leader means attending to your relationships, which comprises a much more complex and nuanced skill set: fostering trust, gaining buy-in, and having consistent, clear, and transparent conversations.

No one tells you that there is an unwritten part of your job description as a leader. At the highest levels of the organization, there is an implicit list of skills required to succeed, skills that you've likely spent little time developing. It was most likely your ability to execute that drove your progress and promotions until now.

Unfortunately, the technical skills that catapulted you to Founder, C-suite or VP, aren't the ones you need to make it in those roles. At the highest echelons of power, relationships are your currency. (If it is unclear what I mean when I say that, you can go to my blog at mettaworks.io where I unpack this idea in detail.) Your mastery of interpersonal skills is what is rewarded. It is what determines your success, or failure, as a leader.

In order to achieve successful relationships, however, you first have to attend to the relationship you have with yourself. This is what I mean when I say that it's all about you. It is vital to know yourself in order to know how to be successful with other people. The inner work required to accomplish this, and reach the power and influence you want, is what this book is all about.

The fact that Stephanie carried so much on her plate meant that she hadn't yet shared those responsibilities appropriately with her team. This had less to do with her workload and more to do with the way in which she was working through her employees. I wondered what might be going on for her internally that prevented her from handing things off.

"Um, why are YOU doing all of that?" I asked when Stephanie paused. Her head jerked up in surprise. "Where's your team in all this?"

"Oh, right." She shook her head in self-deprecation. It's Leadership 101. Every leader I've worked with knows delegation is a key stepping stone to being successful. And yet, so very often, they don't do it. "I'll put a process together for the team to execute," Stephanie agreed.

"No…" I countered gently. Old habits die hard. "What if your team put it together for you to react to."

"Okay," Stephanie said hesitantly. She shifted in her chair, her eyes skittering away from mine.

"How are you feeling about this?" I asked.

"It makes sense," she said, her voice trailing off. After a beat, she blurted out:

"So, then, what is MY job? You know, if I'm just telling people what to do?"

"That's it! That IS precisely your job," I said.

Stephanie sat silently as my words sank in. I continued, "To clarify: telling people what to do means coaching them to produce the results you want. Working through people — getting their buy-in, influencing cross-functionally—to get things done."

My voice softened. "This is what your CEO talked about when he hired me to work with you after he'd promoted you to VP. For you to operate at a higher level of leadership. This IS your role. *This* is operating at a higher level."

It sounds simpler than it is. Working through people entails a very sophisticated skill set. It requires shifting from checking the boxes ("stuff done") to paying attention to bigger-picture items and longer-term deliverables, such as strengthening cross-functional partnerships, inspiring your team, and driving forward an aggressive roadmap.

When you've spent a lifetime working hard and basing your worth and value on how much you get done, it can be difficult to switch gears once you are at the executive level. All that pushing and overachieving helped get you to this level in the first place. It's one of many patterns that has likely been highly valued and for which you have been rewarded, up until now. It makes sense that you'd continue to do more of the same.

In an executive leadership role, however, your job is no longer to execute. Your job is to lead your people so that they produce the deliverable. Every leader I've ever worked with, myself included, dances with this concept.

As Stephanie continued to master and implement this concept in our work together, her ability to delegate quickly and effectively increased. As a result, her overwhelm dissipated and time became an abundant resource. With her newfound time and energy, she was able to become a true thought leader within her organization.

Stephanie ended up as a well-known brand ambassador for the company, a high honor and indicative of their deep trust in her. Essentially the company's public face, Stefanie became widely recognized across her industry. Such success was only possible once she shifted her approach as a leader.

If you're reading this, you're already like Stephanie: an established leader working at the highest levels of your organization. You've fought hard to be there. You've invested an enormous amount of time and energy to attain this level of recognition and responsibility. Yet, you know you could be doing this role better.

You're ambitious and internally driven. Showing up as any less than your personal best is not an option for you. You are hungry for more, and want more than a title. You want to be recognized as a powerful leader. You want to enjoy working with your people. You want to know that your name is being dropped, even when you're not in the room. In short, you want to be wildly successful and take pleasure in it. The problem is that you don't know exactly what is missing or how to do better.

You might have picked up this book because you sense that this relationship piece is what you're missing. You know that your work is now through your people, but in actual practice, something gets stuck. What is it that you're not doing? You deeply long to do better. You fiercely want to know how to engage people to do what needs doing, while not feeling exhausted at the end of the day from doing so. You think you know what needs to happen, and yet, it's not working. You feel like you keep hitting a wall trying to master these aspects of your role.

You are not alone. Many leaders share your experience because the reality is, no one talks about the fact that interpersonal relationships are the core of your success as a leader. This skill set (because it is a skill set) is instead treated like some kind of inherent mystique that some leaders have, while others don't.

This assumption that you either have this "it" factor, or you don't, creates a cascading effect. Because of this thinking, no one talks about how to pay attention to your professional relationships, and as a result, no one talks about what gets in the way of cultivating and strengthening those relationships. Consistently, what gets in the way is your own baggage: your backstories, patterns, and traumas.

This baggage shows up in your performance in profound ways. Your backstory, patterns, and traumas don't stay out of your work simply because they are personal in nature. Unconscious stories, unhealed interpersonal conflicts, and untended relationships infiltrate, nestle in and make themselves at home in your work. Work is where your "demons" go to hide.

You also bring storylines shaped by your identity: family history, gender, race, sexual orientation, and religious background, to name a few. This book isn't about these storylines specifically, but rather helps you become aware of and navigate them.

On top of that, the behaviors that get in the way for you as a leader are often habits you have developed at a neurological level. If you don't shift them at this level, then despite wanting to change, you will keep showing up the same way, repeating patterns you know no longer serve you.

It takes a lot of work and an intentional process to shift these behaviors. The results of doing it, however, are immeasurable. Imagine: you could be in the room with any person in a position of power, and easily offer value, show up as yourself, and be sought after for exactly who you are.

If you're like most of the executives I've coached over the years, these are not new concepts. You've already started on the path of doing your inner work on your demons. You may already be familiar with the landscape of your emotions, or have a sense of when your demons show up. You may have been in therapy, worked with an executive coach, or developed a meditation practice. You understand the basic premise: that your thoughts reflect your belief systems and that how you feel inside is often how you show up on the outside.

The patterns you may be working to shift outside the workplace—say, feeling like your voice isn't heard in your relationships, feeling not good enough, or being afraid to authentically speak your truth—those demons can smell that you're working on them. They don't want to die. They love to hide at work.

Even if you're not doing personal development work outside the office, this holds true, perhaps even more so. Although some familiarity with inner work is not a requirement to benefit from this book, if there is a major trauma in your past that you have not yet begun to process in a therapeutic setting, I would suggest getting professional support before attempting the exercises in this book.

Work is the perfect place to deal with your demons because they're already there, in residence. Moreover, the invisible forces of your inner world drive most of what's happening at work, often lying at the root of conflicts and issues. These issues derail you, your people, and your company, returning less-than-desirable results and leaving you feeling out of control and in the dark. Being defensive, pointing the finger, not speaking up when it's appropriate, and playing small are all great examples of when our inner world is driving the bus. The more you deal with your own stuff, the more you stay in the driver's seat, and the better you show up. The better you show up, the less baggage you bring to the table, the more effectively you can lead through your people.

Most people spin their wheels trying to solve a presenting symptom instead of the root of the problem. Even if they're able to smooth things over or untangle a complex people situation, the same issue will show up again elsewhere, in different contexts, because of the deeply entrenched, neurological patterning. Few know how to get to this root cause and truly make the deep internal shifts required to transform and grow.

This is exactly why I created the MettaWorks Method, integrating tools rarely seen in the coaching world to meet those root causes and instill the required skills to make those internal shifts. This approach concretizes what most of us feel and sense already but might not have language for. The MettaWorks Method makes the invisible visible, bringing interpersonal dynamics to light. Once visible, you are able to use this valuable information to be a powerful and successful leader.

When you have a healthy relationship with what is going on inside you, you have a much larger capacity for the demands of your professional role, and your performance advances dramatically. In the pages to follow, I'll provide tools to help you engage with your inner world so that you can successfully navigate your outer world.

This book, and the MettaWorks Method, is about becoming the sought-after leader you deeply desire to be. When you pay less attention to execution and more to your relationships, you are more successful. It's as simple as that. It is because you work less hard that you are a better leader. In fact, the work is entirely different. As you become fluent in your inner world, you are able to identify unhelpful historical belief systems and replace them with constructive ones. You are able to shift old habitual responses to difficult interpersonal relationships. You create new behaviors that are more skillful and adept. As a result, you are able to see the big picture of your role. You are able to make informed decisions, and you are able to move quickly and strategically because you have a larger perspective and you are not bogged down in the day-to-day details.

In the pages to follow, you'll meet peers and colleagues just like you, who have made it to the upper echelons of their organization. They long to be wildly successful and happy while doing it. They, like you, want to feel confident in the decisions they make and the way they navigate their day-to-day. You'll see how it is possible to change the way you engage your people and how it changes everything.

You'll meet Suni, the CMO who wanted to become an industry leader and sounding board, sought after beyond her company, but her sharp elbows were getting in the way. She was so difficult to work with, people actively avoided her. "I just have a high bar, and no one can handle it."

You'll meet Jonas, the CTO who wanted to be seen as a true thought partner and equal to his peers. Yet he remained stuck in the weeds rather than increasing his impact through cultivating relationships across the company. He secretly loathed what he considered politics at the highest levels and worried, "Is this really my role now?"

You'll also meet Tara, stepping into the coveted role of CEO. She deeply desired to walk into any room with the associated gravitas of a leader in her position—yet fought an urge to flee. "How am I supposed to step it up as a CEO when all these people are demanding so much from me?"

Through the stories of these and other leaders, you'll learn about how they overcame these challenges and became incredibly successful. They discovered, as you will, that the lynchpin to success is the interpersonal, and that the interpersonal starts with you. The more you're clear in your relationship with yourself, the more you can be clear with others. Over the course of this book, I'll share with you the process I've only ever shared with clients: The MettaWorks Method, a step-by-step to the very skills and inner work you need to cultivate this relationship with yourself, so you can master the interpersonal in your career.

Here, gathered, is the implicit skill set required for you to become the impactful, influential leader you deeply desire to be. People will listen when you speak, inside and outside of your organization. They will seek out and value your advice and counsel. Perhaps most importantly, people will be willing to go to the ends of the Earth for you, even when they disagree with a decision you have made.

This is not a matter of opinion; it's a matter of data:

A study of Fortune 500 CEOs by the Stanford Research Institute International and the Carnegie Mellon Foundation found that 75% of long-term job success depends on interpersonal skills, while only 25% on technical knowledge.[1]

75% of careers fall from their trajectory for reasons related to relational skills, including inability to handle interpersonal challenges; unsatisfactory team leadership during difficult times or conflict; or inability to adapt to change or elicit trust.[2]

Relationship savvy is the basis of nearly 90% of why people are promoted when IQ and technical skills are comparable.[3]

In a study of more than 2,000 managers, 81% of the competencies that distinguished outstanding leaders were related to how well they handled interpersonal dynamics.[4]

Approximately 82% of global companies utilize emotional intelligence tests for executive positions.[5]

Strong interpersonal skills are more than learning how to make small talk with your people. It is more than having the right words to show empathy. It is more than making eye contact to show that you're listening. Superficial tactics can only take you so far.

---

[1] https://www.amanet.org/training/articles/the-hard-truth-about-soft-skills.aspx

[2] http://happycamper.world/2015/04/business-roi-of-eq-training/

[3] https://www.extension.harvard.edu/professional-development/blog/emotional-intelli-gence -no-soft-skill

[4] https://www.ecsellinstitute.com/blog/bid/47840/ROI-of-Emotional-Intelligence-Impact -on-Sales-Team-Accountability

[5] https://mitrefinch.com/blog/eq-future-work/

They're not unimportant, but they are just the beginning. This is as far as many Leadership 101 workshops and coaching will take you. However, as an executive, you need much more than that to fulfill a leadership role in your organization and your industry.

You already know that you should delegate. You've taken workshops on "how to have difficult conversations." You know how to practice "active listening." But are you implementing these best practices? And if you are, why aren't they working?

You could be implementing these best practices and still not getting the results you desire, because as good as these practices are, they're limited. There is an opportunity for deeper work. What might you be missing out on? What if you could be getting so much more from your interpersonal interactions?

Something on the subterranean levels of your psyche is getting in the way, and this book is about understanding what that is. This type of work isn't skin-deep. It literally remaps your neural pathways to allow for a profound and sustainable shift in behavior, leading to greater success. It's not just a cerebral knowing; it's a neurological change in your belief systems at the level of your physiology. This is what allows you to show up differently.

If you are committed to becoming the best leader you can be, a leader who people follow, seek out, and refer to; a leader whose impact and influence change the conversation and direct the organization even when you're not in the room—then you're in the right place.

I know you can do this. I've witnessed hundreds of executives embrace these skills and completely transform their impact at work. You have reached your current level of leadership because you are really good at what you do. Now, it is time. It's time to become great at what you do. It's time to become great and enjoy it.

If you're ready, I've got you; and you've got this.

CHAPTER 2

The Opportunity

"I've learned that people will forget what you said, people will forget what you did, but people will never forget how you made them feel."
—Maya Angelou

When I was an in-house HR business partner at a multi billion-dollar tech company, my role was to support leaders to communicate more effectively with their teams, make organizational decisions, and increase employee productivity and engagement. I loved my job. I was good at it. I was proud of the company I worked for.

I then found myself responsible for identifying and firing 25% of a department, 60 employees worldwide. Five dozen people with families who had worked loyally for us for years. The decision originated from the highest levels of the company and was part of a larger business strategy. It became my responsibility to help the business identify who would be fired based on performance and position. It was also my responsibility to then terminate each employee myself.

The executive who should have been directing the initiative absented herself from the entire process. At the time, I seethed with anger, resenting her for dropping the reins and leaving me to pick up the pieces. I'll never forget sitting in yet another meeting to which she didn't show when a member of the C-suite blurted out, "Who's in charge of this, anyway?!"

To which I replied without missing a beat: "Exactly. Who IS in charge here?"

An audible gasp rippled through the room as I stood toe-to-toe with the senior exec, only third in reporting lines from the CEO. By then, I didn't care about how I was showing up. My relationship with my role had become increasingly fraught. I dreaded going to work each day. My physical health started suffering. My stomach churned as I lay awake at night, spinning anxiously about the next meeting, the next decision, the next person I'd add to the growing list.

It was incredibly difficult and painful for me. The directive behind the termination of all of these employees came from leaders I respected. In this instance, I also disagreed with them. Though cost-cutting was the offered justification for the layoffs, the company was incredibly profitable at the time. I couldn't get behind the reasons the company gave. Instead of the leaders taking responsibility for deciding who should leave, it sat on my shoulders.

How could I reconcile the directive I'd been given with my own inner compass? How could I carry out the task that had landed on my shoulders and still remain true to myself? My sense of loyalty to these long-time employees—people I'd spent years getting to know—made the situation all the more painful. I felt angry, sad for the people I was letting go, and guilt-ridden that I held their fates in my hands. How could I manage my emotions and still proceed with my work without letting my anxiety eat me up inside?

This is a perfect example of the complex path we navigate as leaders. We must have the company's back and represent its values. We must do so while also honoring our internal compass and identifying where and how our values overlap—or in this case, how they don't. I felt I had the company's back without honoring my own inner values, and it was becoming an issue for me.

The night before I was to fire those 60 employees, I did a full prostration for each of them at the altar where I meditate. (I've cultivated a serious meditation practice since age 13.) Honoring each employee by name, I asked that their life go well after their exit. As a Buddhist, this was how I could reconcile my values with the company's values in the moment. One of the foundational principles of Buddhism is to relieve the suffering of all sentient beings whenever possible. I was about to create a lot of suffering, and I wanted to do anything I could to mitigate it.

On the day of the layoff, I stilled my mind and calmed my heart before sitting with each person. At a minimum, I could leave my own pain at the door and be fully present for each individual. It was important to me to see them through this pivotal moment in their lives with as much grace and compassion as I could muster.

In hindsight, I could see how, though unconsciously, I was already orienting to attending to the relationship between myself and these employees. Without being explicit, I had decided the only way to navigate this situation successfully was to do my own inner work, focus on the people impacted, and tend to relationships. If I couldn't change the decision to terminate them, I could honor and connect with each one even before we met. It allowed me to prepare energetically, so I entered each conversation with presence, deep respect, and reverence.

The employees felt the difference and responded accordingly. They expressed how they felt my compassion, gratitude, and respect; they could see that they were still valued, even as I let them go. I could see in real time how the way I approached and prepared for those conversations (doing the inner work) made all the difference in terms of how they were received (tending the relationships).

It was a pivotal moment for me, too. The accolades didn't end with the terminated staff. I was very well regarded after this project. The way that I managed a very senior stakeholder, speaking up in meetings, and advocating for the project earned me a lot of respect across the company and a reputation as a leader in my own right.

Even then, I was already attending to the relationships and being rewarded for it. Now, with years of coaching training and experience under my belt, I wonder how I might have tended to the relationship with the absentee executive differently, bringing her back into the process, rather than making her the focus of my rage and feelings of powerlessness throughout the experience. How might I have better partnered with her to get her more actively engaged in the project? How could I have cultivated a better relationship with her, gotten her support and contribution, and perhaps reduced the load on my shoulders?

At the time, however, the whole situation made it clear to me that the gap between my values and the company's values had become too wide. Despite my successful rise within the company, ultimately, I left.

After I left that organization, I specialized in leadership coaching at two other notable tech companies. There, I continued to gain invaluable on-the-ground experience, giving me insights into the most pressing issues for leaders at every level.

I always knew I wanted to run my own company. After implementing these modalities I'd been trained in, and seeing the results these individuals and their companies were getting, I felt like the opportunity was ripe. I founded my company, MettaWorks, while I still worked in-house, with leadership's blessing, to help other leaders in the industry. As my business grew, it made sense to step into it more fully.

Armed with an executive coaching certification earned at Columbia University, I integrated tools and knowledge rarely seen in the professional world to launch my vision for the executive coaching and leadership consulting company that became MettaWorks. The modalities that I've incorporated into the MettaWorks Method are all modalities I've received direct, in-depth training in. Somatic Experiencing, an evidence-based, body-centered approach to healing, is foundational to my work. I received a 3-year intensive training in this approach founded by clinical psychologist Dr. Peter Levine. Polarity Therapy which has helped me coach leaders in balancing their energy flow and translating it into productive behaviors.

I continue to explore and integrate proven psychotherapeutic processes into the MettaWorks Method, including most recently Inner Relationship Focusing, which emphasizes healing the inner self to unlock greater insight and resilience.

All these methods leverage the brain's power of neuroplasticity. The brain has an incredible ability to shift old patterns and develop all-new connections (neurons) in response to experience. Neuroplasticity is the basis of all learning and growth. Using these methods intentionally and mindfully sets the stage for healthy, effective change at the deepest levels of your brain and nervous system.

Most of the time, the situation we face as leaders is less stark than a massive layoff. Often it is much more gray. However, the consequences can feel just as dire, the responsibilities just as heavy. The strongest path to success is to focus on people as your deliverables, and the only way to do that is to do your own inner work. Combining the modalities I mention above, I've taught clients how to regulate their nervous system and manage the energetics of their relationships. These internal changes have powerfully and sustainably shifted how they show up at work. Clients who couldn't get anyone to work with them became recognized across their industry. Others went from having "sharp elbows" to being sought after for advice and insight.

Mitch, a VP of Product, is a perfect example. Before Mitch came to work with me, he had "sharp elbows," motivating people with harsh words and ultimatums at his high-growth tech company.

"I have high standards. That's just how I get my people to deliver," he would retort in response to any negative feedback he received. He would shoot down others' ideas and demand credit when his own ideas were used. What his colleagues saw as "my way or the highway" bullying behavior, Mitch gruffly defended. He credited his bull-in-a-china-shop approach for his success. Historically, he was right. His behavior had been rewarded in the past. Projects got completed, and deadlines were met. Mitch had steadily risen through the ranks.

Finally, Mitch had a chance at a coveted C-suite role: Chief Product Officer. So much was at stake; this wasn't just a move up for him. What Mitch wanted more than anything else was to become CEO, and this promotion was the required next step to prove himself in a role at this level.

When it became known that Mitch was being considered for the role of CPO, the unfathomable happened. A parade of people, from direct reports to cross-functional peers—some Mitch didn't even know—sent emails to the CEO and signed a petition to advocate against his promotion. Almost the entire company categorically objected to it.

Needless to say, he didn't get the promotion. It was a humbling experience Mitch never wanted to repeat. Not long after, he took a CPO role at another company. That's when he sought help from a coach at MettaWorks.

Failure wasn't an option in this new role. Something had to change. His reputation and performance depended on it. Over the course of several months, I worked with Mitch to look at his belief systems. We examined his definition of getting things done. We helped him manage his anxiety about the deliverable and started the work of cultivating trust in his people. He started to experience first hand that getting it done through his people was much more powerful for him, his people and the organization. He shifted his focus from getting the deliverable done to strengthening his relationships so that those around him could execute effectively instead.

He learned to listen, care about what those around him thought, and include their input into his final decision-making and guidance. He asked questions and trusted his people more. By shifting his focus from deliverables to relationships and working through his people, Mitch changed dramatically.

By the end of our time together, people sought out his opinion, where before they'd avoided it. The CEO chose him as a sounding board before making any major strategic decisions. He was quoted by his peers when he wasn't in the room. The retention on his team was higher than in any other department. Mitch practically became the poster child for how focusing on relationships is key to your success as a leader.

"Rachel, I wish I'd *known*. I wish that when I first got promoted at my last company—I wish someone had just pulled me aside and *told me*."

Although Mitch had originally presented as bristly and sharp-elbowed, he had quickly become a favorite client. His superficially brusque exterior masked a thoughtful, self-reflective human at heart.

"I wish someone had told me what this level of position really required. Literally. Like, as part of the onboarding."

Mitch is not alone in his experience. No one talks about the skills you need to succeed at this level: the interpersonal. As Mitch mastered each step of the MettaWorks Method, he became the type of leader that people wanted to follow. He went from being the one person everyone avoided to being the one sought out for his opinions and advice. Mitch's transformation was not magic or impossible. He is still the same person. He still has the capacity to be gruff when under stress, demanding in the midst of a tight deadline. But that is not what he leads with. Those characteristics no longer define his leadership style. And bonus: Mitch is So. Much. Happier.

His story is emblematic of the power of this work. When you do the inner work, you see your success skyrockets, particularly when you are at the top of your organization. I've had the pleasure of seeing it firsthand time and time again. This is what's possible for you and any leader who is willing to go inside, do the work, and shift how you show up at work, for good.

Relationships are your currency at this level, and your first relationship is with yourself. When you gain mastery in relationships, the world becomes your oyster and your whole reality changes, profoundly.

What does that mastery take? Deep awareness, keen interpersonal skills, and profound shifts in your inner world. That's what this book is all about. Execution is no longer your priority, focus, or job. Diversions like responding to a 9 pm Slack from a direct report, or grabbing a direct report's task to "just" do it yourself, are clever ways of avoiding the real work of being a leader. That real role as a leader has everything to do with cultivating and elevating the relationships with your people.

At the upper echelons of leadership, you're doing a totally different kind of work. You are working through people to get things done, often through people who do not report to you. Your perception and understanding of your role need to change. At the highest levels, these very real, unspoken job requirements make or break your success as a leader. And many people get little practical experience with these skill sets until their work and livelihood depend on them, as Mitch's story so keenly showed.

Some leaders have a knack for these skills; you know it because you've met them. They seem to "get" it intuitively:

When these leaders speak, people listen.

Even in the face of disagreement, people follow these leaders to the end of the earth.

Their people deliver their best and their best people stay for years. People trust them implicitly.

Across the industry, people reach out to these leaders for their counsel and expertise.

When we talk about leadership, this is what high performance looks like. But the skills that produce these results are something we rarely put words to.

To the untrained eye, these intuitive leaders achieve their effect effortlessly. They just have an "it" factor. Folks call them natural leaders. Their people want to follow them. But if you had met them at the beginning of their career or earlier in their life, you would know that most people are not born this way. It takes practice, commitment, and self-awareness to become the sought-after leader you want to be.

For the leaders who do not yet have this skill set, this book will help you discover a completely new world and language that will take you to the next level in your role, and with the bonus effect of a happier life and more satisfying career. For those leaders who have the "it" factor, the book will help you harness these skill sets in an intentional way and maximize your power with them.

Don't be fooled. Developing this "soft," essential skill set is not for the faint of heart. You've got to look at your life and take responsibility for it. You have to get curious about how you show up, and the impact that you have on others. This work requires that you identify the patterns and belief systems that aren't serving you anymore.

This work takes courage, and an already deep sense of inner trust, even if you don't always feel that way. It's an opportunity to be aware and compassionate for yourself, and by extension, for your people.

My intention with this book is to change the conversation about leadership. I want this book to change the way we see this "soft" essential skill set. I want this book to transform how we deal with issues at work, and help change industries for the better, starting with tech.

In these pages, you'll learn the pillars of the MettaWorks Method, a step-by-step process that maps out a path to powerful leadership. These steps help you to shift your focus from your day-to-day execution of tasks to the vital relationships and interpersonal skills that are the real currency of your impact at this level. Remember that in order to cultivate sophisticated interpersonal skills such as influence and buy-in in the face of discord, you must first start with the relationship you have with yourself.

At MettaWorks, we have seen over and over again that the most crucial relationship is the one you have with yourself. Yours is the first perspective to consider. This work is done from the inside out. If you follow it and apply its lessons, you'll begin to see changes in how you show up right away. As you learn these skills, you will adapt them in ways that will build your authentic leadership style. With these newfound skills and clarity on the kind of leader you want to be, you'll create outcomes no one else could have reached in the same way.

I have a team of support, and you need one, too. I am meeting you as an expert because I haven't done it alone. Neither should you. A craniosacral therapist, a body code worker, an (intuitive) copywriter, a business coach, a physical trainer, and many others—most of them energetically inclined—all helped me and thus, contributed to the journey of writing this book.

Each of these people has provided me with a different access point in changing my patterns and behavior. Though the work may never truly be done, our relationship to our old patterns, limitations, and roadblocks change. We know how to better navigate our internal world so that we can show up better for those around us.

This book is one more door to help take you through a powerful journey of your inner world to be successful with those around you. The structure of this book is a reflection of how your journey may look when looking inward, step by step. The journey is not linear; sometimes it is cyclical, even. Consider this book a powerful guide to help you through it. With the tools you're about to learn, there's no limit to how successful you can be.

CHAPTER 3

Identifying Drivers:
Your Anchor in the Storm

"All I can be is me, whoever that is."
—Bob Dylan

"I completely disagree with what the board is asking me to do," Yetunde, CEO and founder of a successful tech company, said. "They're pushing me to hire a more seasoned leadership bench—in other words, they want me to recruit from outside the company." She shook her head.

"Walk me through it," I said. "What about the board's suggestion bothers you?"

For Yetunde, the tech space was more than her career industry of choice. Being able to learn how to code, regardless of access to higher education as a first-generation immigrant from Nigeria, changed her life.

"The premise of this company is to make opportunity accessible to people regardless of their education," Yetunde said animatedly. "If we start recruiting our leaders from outside ... with MBAs, no doubt... What message does that send? *Yes, you can come in, but you can only rise so high. You can learn enough to be on staff, but never a leader.*"

Yetunde exhaled audibly. "I'm feeling a really strong reaction to the board's demands," she concluded. "I don't want to do it, I'm not gonna do it. Period." She folded her arms firmly across her chest, then sighed. "I'll be honest, I've locked horns with the board on this for weeks. I'm exhausted."

"It makes a lot of sense that you are exhausted. And I can understand why you are upset," I said. "When we're at an impasse like that, it can be a good time to connect with the why behind our work. What's really important to you here? What's driving you in this situation? In your company?"

"Rachel, when I came here... Being able to learn how to code set me up for a career, for success, for all of this," she gestured around her office, visible behind her on the screen. (Yetunde, like most of my clients, meets with me virtually.) "It gave me an opportunity to create a life I've always wanted."

"The whole point—my mission, the mission of this company I founded—is to ensure that this same opportunity is made available to others. To teach young people of color how to code. To make underrepresented people feel welcome and included so that they can be as successful as possible in a tech environment. That is what is important to me." She was not alone in her passion for the mission; her company had grown to be wildly successful, very quickly.

"And," Yetunde mused, "It's also important to me to do this on a large scale. We've grown so much in the last year, and I do want to grow it over the next few... We do have a dire need to grow the leadership team, I must admit. So, the board's suggestion is not a bad one, it's just... Misaligned."

"So, one of your values is making opportunity accessible and available. And, another of your values is growing and scaling the business for bigger impact," I reflected back. "Where might these values overlap? What might be a solution in this scenario where they're not in conflict? Play with imagining what it would look like to get to honor both of those values in the time between our next session."

Yetunde and I met again two weeks later. As soon as her face appeared on the screen, I could tell she was excited. "I thought a lot about why the board's push to hire outside bothered me so much. I kept asking myself how to align getting a strong leadership

bench with my mission... and I realized that making the opportunity available to everyone goes beyond teaching people to code."

"There needs to be a pathway for people to not only learn the
technical expertise, but for the brightest stars to learn the skills
to move up *within* the company," she went on. "I'm open to what
the board has to say—as long as we also support a fast track program for high-performing individuals so that we can begin to hire
leadership from the inside. The program would prepare them to
become our executive leadership bench."

"I want to set up some roles to always and only be recruited from
within the company," Yetunde added. "If the board agrees, I am
willing to meet them halfway and hire the most urgent leadership roles from the outside. Let's develop the internal leadership
track... and hire for those two roles in the meantime."

What a beautiful solution to a seemingly intractable problem.
Yetunde reconnected to what mattered most to her and, as a
result, came up with a creative solution that met the pressing
needs of her company while deeply honoring her values.

"I know I'm making a difference," she said, after we laid out a
strategy for Yetunde to approach the board with her proposal.
"Reminding myself of the why behind my work, anytime stuff like
this comes up inspires me. I am actually excited about the board
meeting now."

When things got really difficult at work, her mission kept Yetunde
going. Whether they were running out of runway or, as in this
case, the board was demanding that she take the company in a
direction she disagreed with, Yetunde would come back to her
why: Providing underrepresented groups access to new opportunities through coding skills. Learning to code changed the trajectory of her life, and now she gets to offer the same to others.
Her why, even under the most difficult circumstances, allows her
to continue to come from a place of choice.

Fast forward: the board, impressed with Yetunde's suggested solution, approved the leadership track and moved forward with a search for the first two executive hires. As a result of implementing the leadership track program, Yetunde has earned high loyalty with her employees, who perform exceptionally. Turnover is extremely low, rare in her industry. The leadership program has also become a hiring advantage, distinguishing her company in the marketplace and attracting great talent.

All this, because she honored her values in the midst of a conflict with the board. In addition, she was only able to consider potential solutions because of the calm and clarity that identifying her drivers brought. Her values became a touchstone, affording her choice and freedom no matter how challenging the situation.

When we are dealing with difficult situations at work or trying to shift long-standing patterns that no longer serve us and are getting in the way of our success, it can be a veritable storm of conflicting emotions and internal messages. Identifying our drivers anchors us in the storm. Like with Yetunde, when we came back to her why, she had such a clear way to show up to a very difficult situation.

Not all companies are mission-driven. Not everyone is a founder and a CEO. That's why it's so vital to know why you're there, and what you're doing there. What is the bigger picture for you? What is your anchor?

As for myself, as the CEO of my own company, the worst voices pop up in my head to challenge me: What is the point of building a team? Why not stay a small shop and just coach? Even in the writing of this book: Who exactly do I think I am?

Do I realize that by growing my team I'm able to increase my impact, not to mention my income? Yes. Do I know that the tools I'm sharing in this book are highly valuable, and will change lives, just as they've changed the way my clients live and work? Of course. Do the negative voices still pop up? Absolutely. A storm of them. A cacophony. And I engage them. Every. Single. Day.

One of my anchors, my driver, is that I am on a quest. I am on a quest to peel back the layers of my own conditioning, so that I can be the clearest, most pure version of myself. Whether it's through meditation, therapy, energy work, coaching, my company, all of it. Even my family. Someone once asked me, "What made you decide to have children?"

"Because it helps me look at myself," I said. I was embarrassed. I quickly continued, "I guess that's a selfish answer."

My friend said, "What are you talking about? That's a great answer! Most people say, 'I don't want to be alone when I grow old.' Like, they're making companions."

My business, my life, is a conduit to a deep knowing of myself. My husband jokes, "You have no hobbies, Rachel. Your hobbies are working on yourself." It's true; it's what I get excited about.

My company becomes the place where I peel back my personal layers, one by one. It constantly challenges me to look at myself and to meet my deepest, purest, most true self. It includes making good money and having a voice in the industry. Having a successful company means working well with my team, which means dealing with my own stuff every single day.

I have a company to be able to sponsor a life where I can deeply understand myself (through the help of many modalities and experts) and then offer that understanding to my clients and the leadership world. I continue to build my company because it helps me grow.

So what is it that you truly want? What's your why?

To be successful as a leader, you need to focus on your people as your deliverables. And in order to be successful focusing on your people, you need to do your own inner work. The first step in the inner work is knowing your why. Your why is your anchor through your internal and external storms.

The drivers in your work play a profoundly important role in how you show up as a leader. They run deep. They're emotional. And often, they have zero to do with the work itself. Hint: Your behaviors don't necessarily reflect your desires. In fact, sometimes your patterns and behaviors conflict with what you truly want. Example: wanting to be an executive leader but micro managing everything, like Stephanie in the first chapter.

It is important for you to understand your drivers so that you can ensure that your behavior aligns with your intentions. That's why it's so vital to know your underlying intentions, motivations, or drivers, your big why underneath it all. When you encounter a habit that is getting in the way of you getting what you want, you need to have an anchor of: Why does this matter? Why does my work matter?

Staying aligned with your inner drivers—your why—helps you to disrupt behavior that may be getting in the way of achieving your goals. More than that, your inner drivers propel you toward success, toward your ultimate goals.

When you reacquaint yourself with your desire and identify your true North Star, you become powerful. You are aligned and focused on the work required to get you There, wherever There is. When as a leader you know your why, you are less reactive and more responsive, you partner better with others, you make clearer, more informed decisions.

Before doing any other internal work, you need to identify your drivers. Once you understand your drivers, you can decide what you really want. That gives you purpose and the confidence to make good decisions. This is why it is the first pillar in the MettaWorks method.

The problem is that sometimes the drivers aren't obvious. How do you become aware of them? If your inner driver isn't on the tip of your tongue, take a moment to write whatever thoughts or feelings come up from the questions below.

Such questions shine a light on what matters to us:

What's your big, compelling reason for becoming a powerful leader?

How would you spend your days if you had all the money and time you desire?

Where do you feel the most energized during the day (without caffeine)?

What brings you joy?

What kind of impact would you love to have?

Don't worry about getting the answers "right." Consider this a snapshot of a moment in time. It is just to get the wheels turning.

Now, I acknowledge that these questions can be difficult to answer. I've had clients who took a year to get comfortable talking about what they really want. When that is the case, it is important to come back to these questions every time there is a roadblock: "So why does this matter to you?" "What's so important to you about this that makes you want to change?" Sometimes encountering roadblocks help you get clearer on your why. This is often a cyclical process, not a linear one.

Successful leadership at the highest levels is almost entirely dependent on your interpersonal relationships up, down, and across the organization. You can only create strong, trusted, open relationships once you are able to have that same relationship with yourself. When you continue to return to your true driver, it becomes a stronger and stronger anchor in weathering your storms. Ultimately, it informs how you show up every day.

CHAPTER 4

Cultivating Awareness

*"Awareness is like the sun. When it shines
on things, they are transformed."*
—*Thich Nhat Hanh*

Suni didn't hire me. Her co-founder & CEO, who also happened to be her best friend, Rebekah did. The issue: no one wanted to work with Suni. In fact, people actively avoided her. Her team wasn't the problem. How Suni was showing up was the problem. Suni's role as Chief Marketing Officer put her over all things sales and marketing, which was a significant portion of the company. As co-founder, she wasn't going anywhere. Thus, the dire need for a coach.

"It's my resting bitch face,'" Suni joked about the longstanding tension, but the edge in her voice was audible. Seeing her scowl on the screen in front of me, as her eyes dared me to contradict her, I could understand why her team—and everyone at the company, including Rebekah—perceived her as "unapproachable."

Like Mitch in Chapter 2, Suni had "sharp elbows" as a result of her high standards. However, where Mitch was like a wrecking ball in his language and energy, Suni could be seen as more hypercritical and unapproachable—more like death by a thousand cuts. As we dove in deeper to her reactions, she defended her critical attitude toward her direct reports and cross-functional stakeholders. "I have a high bar. If they can't handle it, it's their problem."

She talked a good game, but behind the bravado and frustration, I sensed underlying anxiety. There might even be a sense of helplessness when it came to her team. When they didn't have to be in the room with her, they largely worked as if she wasn't there. The interpersonal strain was slowing the company's progress.

When the company was little more than a start-up of twenty, circumventing Suni was manageable. Most employees interacted with her more affable best friend and co-founder, who passed necessary information along to Suni. But as the company grew, Rebekah didn't have the bandwidth or energy to continue to serve as a buffer for the increasingly alienated Suni.

Now a 90-person organization with $200 million in seed funding, working around one of the two people at the helm was no longer doable. Suni had a team of 4 direct reports and 30 employees, and she needed them (not to mention the rest of the company) to have her back if they were going to make good on their promises to investors: take their company to the next level and hopefully IPO. After receiving consistent feedback from peers and reviews about her style and behavior, Suni was interested in making some changes.

To win the trust and cooperation of her people and to fully engage them, Suni would need to understand how her behavior affected other people. In order to understand her behavior, she first needed to know where it was coming from.

It was important that we get to the root of the behavior that alienated her team. To do that, Suni needed to shift her mindset and understand that interpersonal relationships are her first priority at this level. To fully embrace that people are her deliverables, she needed to start with her relationship with herself. To cultivate her relationship with herself, she needed to become aware of what was going on beneath the surface. This is the second pillar in the MettaWorks method. Specifically, she was going to need to become aware of her inner world.

"Okay, so you're getting this feedback. Your people do not feel supported by you," I said. "What is usually an indicator when that's happening?"

"I'm not sure," Suni admitted.

"Let's talk about the most important meetings that you have during the day. What do you notice about how people respond to you?"

"I feel like I am often getting into arguments. It's not intentional. I'm just bringing an alternative point forward or trying to, you know, raise the bar in terms of our thinking and performance. Which is my job!" Suni's voice started to rise.

"I hear that, and I get it. You don't intend to pick a fight. Let's pay more attention to those moments when you feel like people are getting defensive."

"Let's start with the moment in the conversation you can tell it has gone off the rails," I continued. "All of a sudden, you're in an argument. Usually, the other person's body language or tone of voice is telling you they're unhappy. How can you tell something's not working?"

Suni remembered her last meeting. "Now that you mention it, I was suggesting a different approach to Darnell—different to the one he was taking—and it was like his eyes changed. They got distant, closed off to me... Does that make sense?"

I nodded. Suni continued. "He got really quiet, and it almost felt like he left the room, even though he was still there physically." Her head tilted in concentration.

"Yeah. In the conference room, we have these office chairs that spin, you know? And without getting up, he started to turn away from me. Like he couldn't get away from me fast enough."

Suni started to chuckle, a little painfully. "Yeah... that wouldn't have been the first time." I could see she was starting to see a pattern.

"Okay. So now we need to start collecting data around what you are doing in those moments. Right before Darnell shifted in his chair, what were you thinking? And what was it you said? We need to be aware of how your thoughts impact your words. The clearer we are here, the better we can change how you show up."

Suni's eyebrows flew up. It hadn't occurred to her that this behavior could actually be within her own control.

"Pay attention to what you are saying or doing right before an argument starts. What do you notice about your thoughts at that moment? Just pay attention to that this week. This is the data collection phase. We'll talk about it in our next session."

There are unseen influences that play behind the scenes of all our interactions. And until we learn to pay attention, starting with self-awareness, those unseen forces are in the driver's seat, moving us to behave or react in ways that seem outside our control. These unseen forces could be belief systems we cultivated early in childhood, judgments and assumptions about others, and often fears that we are afraid will bear fruit. Here, Suni's unseen forces were her constant concern that people weren't doing their best and her belief that it was her responsibility to raise the bar on performance through criticism and pushback.

In this chapter, you'll learn how to pay attention to what's going on beneath the surface without being immobilized by it. You will learn how to turn these unseen forces into critical information and a savvy partner you can leverage in your leadership.

It all begins with collecting data.

Start with collecting data around what's not working. With Suni, she needed to start observing the moments when people were getting defensive and shutting down around her. In noticing her thoughts, what she was saying, and what was happening in her body, she was able to get a clearer understanding of those unseen forces, an understanding of what is actually going on. Like Suni, as you pay attention and collect this information, your self-awareness will grow.

Cultivating awareness of our inner world isn't something we're typically taught to do. Most often, we go through our day acting impulsively. Rarely do we pause to get curious about if our thoughts are true or an accurate reflection of what is going on around us. Rarely do we pause to pay attention to what's actually happening versus what we believe is happening. But it is possible to develop this awareness. This is the required next step in the inner work.

I first discovered how to develop this awareness through medi-tation. As a practicing Buddhist, I've had a committed meditation practice since age 13. Meditating taught me that an inner world exists. It allowed me to see my thoughts as separate from myself and recognize that they aren't always true. That was especially important when it came time to define myself outside the expec-tations of parents, peers, and others around me.

This is not a one-and-done realization, by the way; cultivat-ing awareness is ongoing, daily work. Part of my own self-de-velopment has included participating in week-long silent meditation retreats. Keyword: silent. The silence is so fundamen-tally important because I'm alone with my thoughts. I can't justify my inner thoughts and reactions as being caused by someone else. It becomes clear that I create my own reactions from my own thoughts. There's nothing to grasp onto.

I can try, of course. I can fixate on the person sitting next to me breathing loudly, or become incredibly annoyed with the person snoring in the dorm at night. And it's much easier to watch those thoughts spin out and reveal themselves as nothing but thoughts—judgments, really—as the silence continues. I'm left with the reali-zation that no one is making me have those thoughts. Rather, I am the sole creator of my own thoughts.

On one such meditation retreat, I noticed that I spent the whole week waiting for someone to yell at me. At the time of the retreat, I was married and at a point in my relationship with my husband where everything out of his mouth felt like criticism. As the week progressed, I witnessed the thoughts parade through my head: I'm doing this wrong. I'm walking with my hands wrong. I'm not enlightened enough. If I were, I wouldn't be having these thoughts. And on and on, blah, blah, blah. Because it was so silent and because I had no responsibilities or interactions—all I had to do was get up, sit on a cushion at the right time, eat at the right time—realization finally dawned: This is all me.

It was day five when I finally noticed it. No one was saying anything to me, no one was criticizing me. I was doing nothing wrong. The criticism was all happening in my head. Wow. My default is to assume I will be criticized. And if I am assuming this here in silence, what am I assuming with my husband?

It felt like such a profound moment of awareness, one I might not have noticed otherwise. Was my husband always criticizing me, or could he simply be making observations? Quick hack: if you notice the words "always" or "never" in your thoughts, it's pretty much a guarantee that they are false.

It's a very different scenario from being at work, hearing a comment, and feeling triggered and underappreciated. There's no lengthy silent contemplation that allows that thought to spin out or reveal itself to be untrue; instead, most of us stay in that state of reactiveness with little awareness. I'm not saying everyone should meditate or go on a silent meditation retreat; it has been my path toward accessing my own awareness and sense of personal responsibility. Yours may be as simple as going through your day and collecting data.

For me, data collection was noticing the thoughts I carried with me, with or without the presence of my husband. For Suni, it was paying attention to what she was thinking and feeling in the moment when a conversation with a direct report started to devolve into an argument. Just paying attention to your thoughts, and what's happening in your body is what I mean by collecting data. That data leads to cultivating awareness, which is the second step in shifting how we show up through the MettaWorks method. First, identifying drivers; second, cultivating awareness. The point of cultivating this awareness is reclaiming leadership over ourselves. Once we have sovereignty over our own behavior, we can powerfully lead the people around us.

An early deepening in my own awareness began around the time that I was sixteen. Certain events snowballed, and I physically collapsed. I happened to get mononucleosis at the time, which led to staying home for six months. I stopped going to school. And because I'd tested well and was already an A student, I didn't technically have to go.

The issue was, I couldn't rally myself. I couldn't seem to pull myself out of the hole I had fallen into. My mother sent me to work with a highly respected psychoanalyst, Dr. Irwin Hirsch. Psychoanalysis is a therapeutic approach that favors the deep dive, acknowledging that most of our behaviors are driven by the unconscious.

Even after all of these years, I can still remember the exact words Dr. Hirsch used at the end of my first session. Dr. Hirsch complimented me. "You're delightful." Which made me feel all warm, seen, and appreciated, right? Wrong. It was the opposite. In the next session, I didn't say a word. Not a single, solitary word for the entire 45-minute session; we sat there in silence. And Dr. Hirsch patiently, silently, waited it out. It was brutal.

I completely shut down. I realized that during the whole previous session, I'd been doing what I always did: perform. I shut down because I didn't want to say another word unless it was me, really me, and not Rachel disappearing behind a performance. I literally didn't know how to show up as myself.

When I returned for the next session, Dr. Hirsch remarked, "I saw that my words affected you. Can you tell me more about that?" Despite feeling deeply anxious about exploring this, I started to think out loud about why what he had said made me completely shut down. I realized that I felt like I always had to be "on good behavior."

I was always the good girl. I was the one who played mediator in a volatile home environment. I was the one who did so well in school that I was permitted an extended absence without repercussions.

I was the one who delights. Growing up, there was a lot of conflict in my home. To be loved, to keep the peace, I'd learned that I always had to be on my best, most perfect behavior. Always. Getting good grades, being nice, being agreeable. And it worked.

There were a lot of rewards for being good. I was well-liked, and I did well in school. I caused no ripples. I always said yes. I was "nice." I became incredibly skilled at reading a room and managing interpersonal dynamics at school, with friends, and even with difficult teachers. Find the authority figure with the hardest edges, and I was their favorite.

This survival mechanism had other consequences as well. I always worried that I wasn't good enough. My personal boundaries were permeable, nearly nonexistent. The incessant pursuit of perfection made me rigid and inflexible. I started to have crippling TMJ in high school and stomach issues that followed me into my early twenties.

My reaction to Dr. Hirsch's initial compliment revealed that for me, speaking meant performing. I did not know how to speak as myself. I only knew how to show up as others wanted me to. And so, in therapy, where I was supposed to show up as my most authentic self, the only way I knew to do that was to shut up.

Talk about a new awakening. With the tools of meditation and therapy, I began the work of shifting those underlying patterns and beliefs. Becoming aware of the patterns was critical before I could change how I showed up.

At Suni's next session, she shared the data she'd collected that week: how her meetings had transpired and what she thought before she spoke. As we talked through the various conversations of her week, a pattern emerged. Often, when offering feedback to a team member, she'd start with something positive and follow it up immediately with "*but...*"

"This is great, *but...*"

"Good work, *but...*"

"You're on the right track, *but...*"

This pattern became low-hanging fruit for an immediate, quick fix that—though superficial—could begin to shift how these conversations ended.

"Do you notice how 'but' negates everything that comes before it?" I pointed out. "When people hear that, they fixate on the 'but,' and it sounds like the initial 'compliment' was just padding. The compliment seems insincere."

Suni's eyes widened. Her intentions were sincere. At the same time, she felt she needed to help raise the bar. As a result, her language reflected that.

"So let's start there," I advised. "This is a simple change you can make: Put a period at the end of that sentence. "As in, 'This is great.' Period. In fact, don't stop there. Add two more sentences about why it's great. And you have to really mean those sentences. The "but" isn't just a language issue. It's an energetic issue. The person can feel your disagreement and criticism. In order for this to work, you need to truly appreciate where they are coming from in your mind and in your emotions. In those moments, really invoke the feeling of pride that you have for your team. Then pause before you offer any suggestions."

Suni nodded thoughtfully.

"Then," I concluded, "See what happens differently."

As Suni implemented this modest change, she saw that it started to defuse some of the tension that had seemed inevitable whenever she had given feedback to her people. We couldn't have arrived at that change until she had cultivated awareness of what was happening in her own mind.

Within six months and a lot of work walking through the steps of the MettaWorks method, Suni had evolved from a person no one wanted to work with, to someone they sought out for advice and opinion. In fact, her 360 feedback reflected that. One of her colleagues said, "I don't know what happened to the old Suni—but I love the new one, and I hope she's here to stay."

Awareness is the critical next step toward transformation, and a critical tool toward awareness is collecting data.

Now it's your turn.

Awareness provides insight. When you cultivate awareness, you have immediate and valuable information that you can use. You'll shift from reactive to proactive in responding to any situation and feel more in control of what's happening.

You start by identifying what is not working. Then you collect the data, paying attention to yourself and the circumstances. The data will start to point to your deeper patterns.

Take a moment to think about a challenging situation at work. Set a goal around collecting data on that situation this week.

When you're reflecting on the difficult situation, get curious about:

What happened right before the moment when things got challenging?

What thoughts were running through your head?

Where else do you see these kinds of thoughts arising? What do those situations have in common?

How were others responding to you in word and body language? How did you feel?

What was your body telling you?

Note if or when:

You felt suddenly frustrated, anxious, or experience an unwarranted sense of urgency.

Your chest felt tight or constricted.

Your pulse started to race or pound.

Your palms sweat.

You felt foggy or unable to focus on what someone else is saying.

By cultivating self-awareness, you'll begin to notice when these signs are visible aspects of patterns that affect how you're interacting with your people. Your newfound awareness creates an opportunity for an entirely new way of being.

CHAPTER 5

Reading the Room

*"The most important thing in communication
is to hear what isn't being said."*
—Peter Drucker

"My Chief Operating Officer is presenting to the board next week. Just like we planned." The founder of a fast-growing biotech company, Andrew, had been working with me for three months when he made this announcement, visibly uncomfortable.

Andrew had hired me to help him intentionally scale his team. That team included the new Chief Operating Officer. Before passing the baton, Andrew himself had been solely responsible for Operations.

His company was growing quickly and had completed a round of funding that had allowed them to expand. He had been in charge of Product, Marketing and Operations and thus the main executor before hiring his new leadership bench. With a new team, Andrew was working on how to empower his people effectively. It was time for him to pull out of the weeds and focus on the longterm strategy for the company. He had hired a terrific leadership bench as a result of the work we had done together. Now, it was going to be the new COO's first presentation to the board.

"How do you feel about that?" I asked, even though Andrew's body language already spoke volumes. He was making only cursory eye contact, he fidgeted in his chair, and his voice was half its normal boom.

"I'm worried," Andrew admitted, shaking his head as if to try to rid himself of the anxiety. "I mean, I should be relieved. This is what we worked toward! It's not my COO; I trust him. His work has been nothing but fantastic so far. I just—" Andrew hesitated, and I nodded, encouraging him to go on.

He continued abruptly, "It's—the board is going to look at me like, *And what do YOU do now, Andrew?*" He absentmindedly crossed his arms and rubbed his hands against his sleeves. He was more nervous than I'd ever seen him.

"I'll just be sitting there, like some kind of figurehead," he said. "I wanted this, right? So why am I feeling so...?" Andrew squeezed his arms, rolled his eyes, and exhaled a sigh of frustration, leaving the sentence unfinished.

"Okay. So, I hear you saying you're not sure the board will still value you or your input," I said. "Well, how can you tell? At the meeting, I mean?"

Andrew looked at me blankly. Normally an intuitive guy, I knew he wasn't purposely being obtuse; his anxiety about this changing of the guard was getting in the way of him leveraging his intuition. We'd worked together long enough that he had already cultivated a level of self-awareness, so I started there.

"You remember, a couple of sessions in, when I had you collecting data?" I asked.

Andrew nodded; by now it had become second nature for him to notice his thoughts and feelings over the course of the day, especially in the moments right before something went off the rails—or was going particularly well. The next step was helping Andrew to cultivate and apply those skills to better read the room, specifically the spoken and unspoken signals people send.

I advised Andrew, "This week's assignment is to collect data again, specifically at this board meeting. Pay attention to how the board reacts to the new COO and to you. There's nothing you need to say or do. Just observe." Andrew nodded, grimly determined to keep his cool until then.

At an executive level, people will rarely say to your face what you're doing right or wrong or how to win their buy-in, confidence, and cooperation—if they are even able to articulate it in the first place. You need to learn how to read the room to gather that important feedback and trust the information you're gathering in this way.

Your ability to read the room eliminates self-doubt. It allows you to trust how you read others' reactions as information without needing explicit feedback. This is the next level of cultivating awareness: first of self, next of interpreting others' unspoken signals. Reading the room is the next fundamental pillar in the MettaWorks method. What are those unspoken signals? They are implicit feedback, telling you how you're performing. It's the next stage of developing awareness.

Andrew's unfamiliarity with the concept of implicit feedback is not unique. Once upon a time, you received annual performance reviews that told you how you were doing, a.k.a. explicit feedback. As you got higher up in your organization, those turned into 360 evaluations which may or may not have contained helpful feedback. These 360 evaluations happened once a year if you were lucky, and sometimes completely disappeared if you were unlucky.

At the executive level, there are fewer people with a complete view of your work and fewer still who can tell you how they really feel without risking blowback. For example, if you're a CTO, your engineering VP may not tell you that you are difficult to work with. Conversely, your only clues as to whether your peers are confident in your ability to lead may be in the conversations they choose to have with you. The feedback will come through their actions, such as whether they seek you out for advice or whether they lean in and engage with what you have to say. Thus, in order to gauge your performance, you need to look for clues in your relationships. You have to look past the superficial. You need to look past your own feelings or internal stories, as Andrew was learning to do, and start to observe how others react to you.

Leaders receive a constant stream of these cues. They can signal great opportunities or warn you when it's time to change course. Unless you actively pay attention to this implicit feedback, however, you may never reap the benefits of reading the room. You need to learn to interpret what's being communicated without words so that you are able to understand the underlying concerns and emotional responses. When you respond with an understanding of where people are coming from, it is easier to get your people on board, nurture advantageous partnerships, and resolve conflict.

This requires becoming aware of people's signals. Once you can read the signals, you'll next need to learn how to translate them. What are people's responses saying about you and your effectiveness as a leader?

Growing the company demanded that Andrew expand his leadership team, so he made the important hires. Rationally, logically, this was the right thing to do; but he was besieged by self-doubt. "If I'm not doing the work, what's my job?" Through hiring a leadership bench under him, Andrew created an opportunity to pull out of the weeds, focus on creating a clearer strategy and get the team aligned with that strategy. To do so, he was obliged to operate differently. Remember, his people are his new deliverables, not the deliverables themselves. Gauging his effectiveness as a leader required trusting his ability to read the room. This is the next level of inner work required to become an exceptional leader.

Reading the room accurately can make the difference between a closed deal and a blown negotiation; between building a collaborative partnership, or unwittingly driving a greater wedge in the relationship; between succeeding or failing as a leader.

At our next session, Andrew was beaming.

"How did the—" I barely got the question out before he answered.

"The board meeting went really well."

I smiled. "How could you tell?"

"Well, the COO's presentation was excellent. So—" and here, Andrew looked a little sheepish, "Instead of making me look... I don't know, superfluous, like I was afraid he would, it was the opposite. He made me look good because he was so prepared."

"And then," he continued, his eyes twinkling, "the board had some higher-level strategic questions about the product's long-term financial projections that were beyond the COO's purview. Those questions, I could definitely answer. I still had a purpose there."

I nodded and reminded him about the implicit feedback. "What did you notice? What was happening in the room?"

"As I talked, people were nodding in agreement. They engaged in a high-level conversation with me, including my direct report."

"So what did that tell you?"

"First off, that I hired the right person," Andrew laughed. "The meeting definitely showcased my COO's credibility. And that this is working. I can offer the higher-level vision—in a deeper way than I could when I was presenting on operations, actually. The board was engaged and interested in what I had to say."

"I'm in the right place," Andrew concluded. "I have something to offer beyond being hands-on in the work."

Andrew's ability to read the feedback of the conversation in the boardroom allowed him to develop confidence that his contribution was valued. Interpreting and integrating implicit feedback is crucial no matter if you're like Suni, whose team members were avoiding her, or Mitch, whose organization came out to protest his promotion, or Andrew, who feared he didn't have a role when he was no longer in the weeds.

By understanding the implicit messages that everyone, from your peers to yourself to your CEO, constantly broadcast, you'll be better able to meet people where they are, influence the direction of the conversation, and respond appropriately.

Your success as a leader at the highest levels depends on your relationships across the organization. In an environment where you no longer receive explicit feedback, you can only create strong, trusted, open relationships once you are able to read and interpret the implicit signals your people send you all the time. Just as you worked toward cultivating awareness in the last pillar, in this pillar of the MettaWorks method, you cultivate that awareness of your people's unspoken feedback. It requires trusting your inner compass—otherwise stated, your intuition. In the last chapter, you learned how to cultivate awareness of your own thoughts and patterns by collecting data, and experienced firsthand how the resulting awareness is, by itself, profoundly transformational.

This next tool is another exercise in data collection. This time you are cultivating awareness of your people's unspoken signals, or reading the room. This week, reflect on a conversation or meeting you had, and ask yourself these questions:

What did I notice about the other person's body language and response?

How can I tell when something I said was well received? (Example: Were people leaning in, engaged, asking questions, nodding?)

How can I tell when something I said has not landed? (Example: Are people looking away, fidgeting, silent, or distracted?)

What other cues might signal that it is time to shift my approach?

Each of these questions will alter how you next show up as a leader. This is the power of awareness and reading the room.

Keep in mind that this, and every pillar of the MettaWorks method, entails a skill set that you build over time. I can't and wouldn't give you a list of cues to look for and prescribe how to respond because there are no one-size-fits-all answers. This is why data collection is so important. You learn to observe what's happening in the room when things aren't working, and what's different when they are. As a result, you can intentionally shift your approach, so the latter happens more often.

This is a nonlinear process, more like a spiral. We never stop learning how to become ever more self-aware and how to better read the room. Don't get discouraged if an apparent slip-up follows a victory. If anything, the bumps in the road (and your awareness of them) signal that you are on the right path, the spiral path.

Reading the room is a sophisticated art. Every company, every team, has a unique culture. Each person, including you, has a particular background. What works for one person may not work for another.

As you'll see in the coming chapters, everyone has their own conditioning, survival mechanisms, and baggage. All of these factors can interfere with your developing trust in your instincts, your awareness and your ability to read the feedback you're getting in the room.

Knowing that, cultivating awareness and reading the room will be powerful tool sets for you. You will return to these pillars again and again, seeing how they change the dynamics of your relationships the more you practice.

It doesn't happen overnight. Eventually, with repetition, these skills become second nature. The more you cultivate them, the more people will feel at ease around you. Each time you practice, the more people will feel that they are being heard, met, and understood. They will trust you and be ever more willing to follow where you lead.

CHAPTER 6

Pattern Identification

"We can change the world if we change ourselves. We just need to get hold of the old patterns of thinking and start listening to our inner voices and trusting our own superpowers."
—Nina Hagen

My client Jonas, a Chief Technology Officer, is the one millennial I know who has been at the same company for fifteen years. Making a big impact at a 3,000-person tech company that's well-recognized in the industry, he's moved up in the organization many times.

From the outside, Jonas' newest role, which took him into the C-suite, was a step up in every way. Just three people removed from the top executive in the company, he now headed a team of 300 global reports. He had a larger reach and a higher level of impact than he had ever had before.

Inside, however, Jonas was floundering. For the first time in his career, his anxiety reached an all-time high. Despite his efforts, large initiatives under his leadership were not progressing at speed. Jonas knew he was in danger of losing the promotion.

As a high-performing player, Jonas was nominated for coaching by the executive leadership team. If he played a more strategic role as a leader, he'd be unstoppable. He needed to pull out of the day-to-day details, start communicating the vision for the team, and empower them to execute effectively.

The problem: Jonas was working 18-hour days. Despite such long days, he was not attending to the most important parts of his role. He had yet to put together a business continuity plan that included a customer escalation process so that client issues could be handled without his input. Rather than building and communicating that process, however, he was putting out fires. Jonas was stuck in execution mode.

A perfect example cropped up in a recent session. Jonas had logged in at 12:30 a.m. one night that week to check the performance of the company's network. His wife went looking for him when he hadn't come back to bed. She found him at his standing desk, staring closely at the screen.

"What's going on?" she'd asked.

"Just checking on something at work."

"How bad is it?" She'd witnessed how, in Jonas' previous roles, a downed server could pull all hands on deck, no matter the hour.

"Not bad. Or not bad yet, I should say," Jonas had quipped, proud to have nipped the situation in the bud before it turned into something more serious. His wife was not impressed.

"She just stared at me," he told me, chuckling humorlessly, "before, rolling her eyes, she turned and walked away without saying another word."

"She didn't really need to say anything I heard her loud and clear," he admitted. "'*And for this, you get me up in the middle of the night?*'" They have two young children. More sleep deprivation was the last thing the couple needed.

"So, why were you working in the middle of the night?" I asked.

Turns out, Jonas was on Slack with his team, supporting them as they were troubleshooting an issue with the server, an issue that could have easily been handled by one of his direct reports without his presence. At this level, he no longer needed to be on the computer in the middle of the night unless things were really dire. In fact, it wasn't just unnecessary, it was completely unscalable.

He was in charge of a huge organization and could not be up at midnight every time a server had an issue. Jonas being up late on Slack for something so minor meant he was far too deep in the weeds.

Work was a constant source of stress for Jonas. He felt like he always had to answer Slack messages, no matter if it was an evening or weekend, even though he had a team of people rotating on-call. Once upon a time, as an individual contributor and even as a manager, he had been expected to always be "on call." He had been directly responsible for putting out fires like a downed server. That's not to say that there isn't an existing culture at some tech companies that demand all team members remain "on call," 24/7, no matter their level—but that unreasonable expectation is not what I'm speaking to here. Although his ability to execute undoubtedly contributed to Jonas' rise through the ranks, this habit or pattern of behavior—going into execution mode—was no longer helpful in his current role. It was not scalable and it was unsustainable. If he was up monitoring every issue that arose he would literally never sleep.

Jonas was investing time and energy in tasks that were better delegated. This meant that there were other issues, projects, and relationships requiring his attention that he was actively avoiding. This was the real issue getting in the way of his being effective in his role and responsibilities. Jonas' avoidance of the more important aspects of his role would eventually relieve him from said role if he didn't turn things around. He was stuck in a pattern that not only no longer served him, it was actively impeding his success. In order not to drop any balls, he was working an unsustainable schedule. And even with all the time invested, the larger initiatives the CEO was looking to him to direct were moving at a glacial pace. He constantly worried that he just couldn't cut it at this level.

When I pressed him about why he was up in the middle of the night doing something his team should be doing, he paused, then conceded in a soft voice, "I just can't seem to turn it off." Pattern identified.

We all know the quote Einstein is credited with saying, that doing the same thing over and over again and expecting a different result is the definition of insanity. But what if you're not aware that you're doing the same thing over and over again? This is why identifying patterns, and continuing to become aware of them, is so critically important to shifting the behavior that we want to change. Hence why it makes up the next pillar in the MettaWorks method.

Unhelpful behavioral patterns obfuscate what we want to avoid. They allow us to continue not looking at the deeper emotions or beliefs that are driving the pattern in the first place. When we understand our patterns and how we create or perpetuate those patterns we can then change how we show up—and our results.

The good news is that Jonas was aware that there was a pattern and that it was hampering his ability to lead effectively. I congratulated him on his insight and invited him to celebrate it. "You are noticing that you can't shut it off. That's an important awareness." I paused, then continued. "See how you're prioritizing something that someone on your team can do? This is the direct opposite of you having a more strategic role. What do you think is happening here?"

"Well... I know how to fix the server." Jonas spread his hands helplessly. "It's that satisfaction of a job well done, you know? I know exactly what the criteria for success are. In my current role..." he paused. "Not so much."

As the liaison between the product and the compliance teams, Jonas needed to work in partnership with his peers, other top level executives at his company.

Like many at his leadership level, Jonas was caught by surprise when the nature of his work changed from managing deliverables to leading through relationships. Now being successful meant working with people across the organization in order to get those same deliverables completed. It's not that Jonas wasn't good with people. On the contrary, he understood how to do this work with his direct reports. They felt heard, his priorities were clearly expressed, and the team executed successfully. As a result, Jonas' team was fiercely loyal and got behind any initiative he put in front of them. He loved his team.

However, Jonas hated having to manage cross-functional relationships with his peers. Interactions at the peer level demanded that Jonas sit in his authority without leveraging the comfort of a reporting structure. He needed to stand confidently and influence his peers, engage in difficult conversations, and foster agreement and alignment on varying initiatives. "Moving chess pieces," as he put it, partnering, and driving buy-in took Jonas into unfamiliar waters. He couldn't just tell his colleagues what to do, especially the ones who outranked him, few as there were.

"These relationships feel so... amorphous." Jonas shook his head. "How am I supposed to manage them?" His peer relationships required a whole new level of nuance and skill as well as rock-solid confidence in his being an equal at the table.

As we scratched below the surface of Jonas' pattern, we uncovered that he had a fear that he didn't belong, that he didn't have what it takes to lead at this level. In short, he felt inadequate. "I don't know how to do my job now," he admitted shyly. For Jonas, the pattern of going into execution mode, over and over again, allowed him not to look at these uncomfortable feelings of inadequacy.

Jonas' homework was to start paying attention when he felt anxious, cultivating his awareness with the same data collection tools you learned a couple of chapters ago. Specifically, he was to note when he felt anxious versus when he didn't, and when he felt confident: in his decision-making, his performance, and how he showed up with his peers.

Jonas began to notice when his thoughts ran on a loop in the middle of the night, urging him out of bed—and toward some totally justifiable (and totally delegatable) task. This was the red flag that he was orienting to execution mode rather than strategic mode.

By shining a light on this specific pattern, Jonas could see how he avoided uncomfortable feelings by burying himself in busywork. As we dug deeper, he could see how defaulting to execution mode covered underlying anxiety around his contribution. Defaulting to execution mode allowed him to not have to ask himself the deeper questions of "Who am I? What is my true value?" Until Jonas was aware that he was stuck in a behavioral pattern, work was going to continue to stress him out. He was going to continue avoiding stepping into the strategic role for his team, which was the very reason he had been directed to work with me. If he didn't shift this pattern and step into a more strategic role, he was going to lose this latest promotion.

Through this awareness of the pattern, Jonas started shifting his behavior. When his hands started itching to jump in on one of his team's technical projects, he learned to catch himself, let his team handle it, and ask himself instead, "What am I avoiding right now?"

Implementing these changes were an important step. By continuing our work together in coaching, and leveraging the pillars of the MettaWorks method, things have totally changed for Jonas in his work. He has become a strong thought partner in the room with his peers. Jonas now sees his role as developing strategic initiatives and strengthening communication with his peers in order to remove roadblocks and allow his team to move as effectively as possible.

He continues to work on clarifying how he wants to communicate. He's getting clearer on what success looks like in his role and therefore cultivating trust in what he has to offer. He is becoming the sought-after leader he always wanted to be.

Today, peers come to him for advice on how to foster the same loyalty with their teams that Jonas inspires in his. His strategies are being shared as benchmarks for verticals of the company outside his scope of responsibility. The more he takes the lead on conversations involving his functional area, the more engaged his fellow C-suite executives have become. As a result of his strategic leadership at work, he is getting his life back at home, relaxing in the evenings with his family and enjoying long sleep-filled nights. None of that was possible without identifying the pattern that was keeping him stuck.

Unhelpful patterns can show up anywhere in our work and lives, and they always mask important hidden beliefs or stories that must be brought to the surface. For example, one of my own patterns impacts my relationship with my husband. He is the cook in the family. Not only does he enjoy it, but he is also really good at it. After long days working, he often comes home and cooks dinner.

For years, without fail, I would walk into the kitchen and criticize how he was preparing the meal, such as his method of chopping vegetables. (I like my veggies chopped a little smaller than bite sized, okay? But—I digress.) It was a pattern that I repeated so often and so consistently that it actually became a running joke between us. He'd see me walk into the kitchen, and before I had a chance to open my mouth, he'd predict my words and say them before I had a chance to:

"You're doing it wrong!"

My husband was unknowingly and playfully giving me the gift of pattern identification. This pattern prevented me from simply receiving and enjoying a delicious meal cooked by my husband. And although we laughed about it, I also didn't want to continue criticizing him while he was doing this wonderful thing for our family. I wanted to be an appreciative partner, not a critical one. Once the pattern was identified, so playfully and lovingly by my husband, I began the work of disrupting it, which you'll hear more about in the next chapter. Just like Jonas, I couldn't even begin that process until I identified (with a little help) that this was an unhelpful behavior pattern in the first place.

As you begin your own work of identifying patterns, suspend judgment. Notice them lightly, in a spirit of curiosity or even humor. Patterns that were once helpful, such as Jonas' default to executing when he was an IC, can become harmful when they no longer serve us. That shift doesn't mean there's something wrong with you. Patterns are human. In fact, some are even helpful, like driving a car, where we can do it without even thinking about it. However, it is important to shift the ones that have become unhelpful to us. Good intentions are always the driver behind any pattern we've developed. They have been created to protect us, but when they stop serving us, it becomes time to change them.

We all need help in identifying our patterns, whether it is with a coach or a partner. We cannot do this work alone. The next step is truly to get the support you need in your life to help you do so. The following tool is a way to start.

Jonas' old pattern was defining execution as a job well done. In fact, at some point, he learned that his very survival depended on it. That's why your patterns are to be treated with respect, curiosity, and even reverence. There is wisdom in the pattern, a reason why the pattern commenced in the first place. The intention is right—but the wisdom is outdated.

The more deeply entrenched the pattern, the more likely that it stems from a survival mechanism that served us well in the past. In a later chapter, we'll talk more about these mechanisms and how to tell when or under which circumstances their wisdom is harming more than helping. We identify patterns so we can start to get to the hidden stuff underneath, the mechanism behind the pattern. Identifying your patterns allows you to step back and recognize that you have a choice. You have the freedom to choose whether or not you follow the pattern.

Now it's your turn to apply what you've learned.

Identify a recurrent pattern of response, feeling, or behavior. A good place to start is an area where you feel trapped or stuck in a rut. A great way to identify a pattern is to look at those behaviors that you feel you "just have to" do but aren't doing yet.

Examples: "I just have to get to the gym." "I just have to delegate more." Notice how "I just have to" means you're not doing it now.

What behaviors are getting in the way of achieving what you want?

This is the next step toward long lasting sustainable change, and the next pillar in the MettaWorks method. To succeed in your interpersonal relationships, the true nature of your work as a leader, you must know yourself and your patterns. Without this inner work, you will continue to be tripped up by habits and repetitive behaviors. Remember that Jonas couldn't embrace the skills he needed as a leader until he identified and dealt with his pattern of losing himself in operations.

Buckle your seatbelts. In the next chapters, you'll head into the deep end of the pool. You will get to understand and befriend your inner world in a much more sophisticated way, becoming clearer in the survival mechanisms and stories behind the patterns. Get ready to turn the invisible visible and stand in the true power of your leadership.

CHAPTER 7

Disrupting Patterns

"When patterns are broken, new worlds emerge."
—*Tuli Kupferberg*

"Get me out of here, Rachel."

On track to step into the CEO role of a 500-person organization as its founder stepped down, Tara felt profoundly conflicted about the move. She was torn between feeling confident that she could do a better job than the current CEO and an overwhelming urge to flee immediately. The reason for the latter became clearer as we worked together.

Tara was more than qualified to be a great leader. She brought experience cultivated over 15+ years. She consistently delivered terrific results and was responsible for strategies that, year over year, strengthened the company's brand and performance in the industry. For anyone who knew Tara, there was no question about her potential for impact far beyond the company. This is precisely why the cofounder had nominated her to succeed him as CEO.

As he passed the baton, he had one piece of important feedback: Tara needed to assert herself more powerfully, be more directive and stand boldly in the role of CEO. This was when Tara reached out to work together. The feedback corresponded to her own observations. Tara agreed; she noticed how she often held back and waited for permission from everyone else before asserting her viewpoint or making a decision. She knew that she needed to own her leadership. She needed to feel comfortable stepping into the role of CEO as the ultimate decision maker.

Tara's experience highlights another theme of the leaders I work with: learning to trust your internal compass with the utmost confidence. Indecision, second-guessing yourself, or turning to others for feedback and validation may be signs that your confidence in your inner guidance is less than unwavering. This same uncertainty had also kept Jonas stuck in the last chapter, immobilized from meeting the expectations of his fellow leaders despite the fact that they had hand-picked him for his elevated role.

Although Tara was stepping into a more prominent role, with more responsibility and higher expectations, she continued to let others hijack her calendar. Here was a leader who was already sought-after, basically in charge of the entire company, even before becoming CEO. Yet she continued to over accommodate others before attending to herself. A perfect example of this was the way she scheduled her coaching sessions. She didn't schedule them during her workday, despite the fact that her company paid for and supported them. It felt like a perfect opening to address the bigger issue.

"Remind me" I said. "Was it because of my schedule that we have our sessions booked after your working hours?" Tara was a few hours ahead, in a different time zone.

"Oh, I don't know," she replied, her voice hesitant.

"What if we changed it to earlier?" I urged. Tara's eyes widened. I could sense the panic starting to rise in her. I watched as she struggled to regain her composure.

"Um, okay," Tara said, now at half her normal volume.

"Hold on," I said. "Let's pause here for a second. I can see this is bringing something up for you."

"I don't know… You know, my schedule is so full. This is the only available time," she said, her voice rising in pitch as she provided a concrete and logical reason why it didn't make sense for us to change our meeting time.

Since we were working on Tara asserting herself in her role and her "in charge-ness," I knew this was a place we needed to hang out. We had already moved through the first pillars of the MettaWorks method, so I knew that I could challenge her a bit.

Tara had complained more than once that people were constantly scheduling meetings on her calendar without consulting her. In allowing this behavior to continue, she had put others and their needs and demands ahead of herself in the use of her time. She overaccommodated her employees and peers instead of letting them know the parameters of her calendar. No wonder she wanted to "get out of here." Letting everyone else be in charge of her day and deliverables was totally overwhelming her. This behavior was the antithesis of inhabiting the CEO role.

If Tara were less overwhelmed, she'd be able to implement decisions more effectively. She wouldn't want to get out; she'd want to dig in. The pattern here was that she felt she couldn't assert herself as the decision maker. If she created boundaries in her calendar, with someone protecting it and managing it, she could choose to spend her time in the most valuable way. She would be creating and communicating the company's larger goals and therefore operating at the level of CEO. Happily, as a result, she would also be drastically less overwhelmed. The more time and space she had, the less she would wish to flee.

However, before we could shift the pattern, we needed to disrupt it. We needed to stop the pattern from repeating itself. In doing so, Tara and I could understand what was underneath the pattern, and why the pattern existed in the first place.

"What if we said that we're moving all our sessions to your normal working hours, starting tomorrow? This is hypothetical; we're not changing anything right now—but I want to hear your initial reaction when I suggest it."

Tara rocked back in her chair, blinking rapidly. "I don't feel like that's okay," she said. Tears began to course down her cheeks.

Her eyebrows flew up, shocked by the rapid escalation of her emotions.

This pillar of the MettaWorks method, disrupting the pattern, isn't about making a change. This step is about noticing what happens when you *stop* the pattern you want to change. Disrupting patterns reveals what your patterns are trying to hide. Data collection is important here. Interrupting a behavioral pattern reveals a great deal of information. That information appears in what happens next, how you feel, what sensations course through the body, and what thoughts arise.

The intensity of Tara's reaction revealed that this pattern around her calendar had deep roots. Patterns with the deepest hidden causes emerge from the very mechanisms you developed to survive, usually as a young person. (We'll explore survival mechanisms further in the next chapter.)

"I don't feel like I can spend my time on coaching during work hours, you know, for my benefit," Tara coughed, blotting her tears with the palms of her hands.

"I can see how upsetting this is for you," I said and nodded sympathetically as Tara calmed. "If it's okay, let's hang out here a little longer. You should know that I don't see my other clients on their weekends or nights. Leaders come to me during their day. Companies *pay them* to see me during their working hours. Right now, it's important to get curious about what you're feeling, to feel what's coming up, and be steady in it. It's important to just witness your level of fear in this moment." I paused.

"Notice that this reaction is arising before we've moved even a single one of our sessions," I finished. Tara's strong reaction was a sign of her deep resistance, an internal obstacle to making a change. Understanding resistance is yet another pillar that we'll explore in more detail later. Before you can dive into resistance and truly shift in a profound, sustainable way, however, the pattern must first be disrupted. You need to understand what the pattern is hiding so that you can solve the root of the problem.

In Tara's case, the vital information from her inner world was the terror she felt in managing her calendar differently. This terror revealed the core reason she was struggling to assert herself as CEO.

"What are you worried about when you think of being in charge of your calendar?" I asked.

"To be honest, the first thought I have is: Who am I? Who am I to tell my people how to fill my calendar? Isn't that my job? To be available and have an 'open door?' What will people think of me if I don't make myself available? Who am I to be CEO?" she completed her thought, seeming to surprise herself with where she landed.

"Ah. Look at that. Look at what was hiding behind a little old calendar. Quite a lot!" I reflected back. "What great insight. The terror of being in charge of your calendar is directly related to your concerns about being CEO."

This is why it's critical to pay attention to even the smallest details and patterns. Tara's pattern around the calendar seemed insignificant, but it became a window into what needed to shift for her to truly embrace her role as CEO.

The visceral nature of your reaction when even thinking of shifting patterns can reveal how deep they go. This is the power of disrupting patterns. Tara was able to see that she had a lot of fear around her asserting her authority, and that fear informed her behavior and put her at the whim of everyone else. Her awareness indicated progress, allowing us to understand the core of the problem. This awareness became a helpful roadmap for our next level of work.

I understood the intense feelings that can arise when disrupting a deeply held pattern. I had felt them myself when I got curious and asked myself, "Okay, what if I kept my mouth shut when I was in the kitchen with my husband?" Here was an opportunity to try and disrupt the pattern of criticizing him whenever he cooked for me (or did anything kind or loving, for that matter).

Here's what I found: it was really hard. And this was about chopping peppers!! Again, seemingly insignificant, yet indicative of a much bigger issue. Imagine the difficulty of interrupting a pattern when the stakes are actually high. I felt this intolerable surge of nervous energy running through my system and deep insecurity the moment I tried to stand in the kitchen and simply allow my husband to cook a beautiful meal for us. The first 10,000 times I tried to keep my mouth shut, I was able to do it for a max of three minutes. Let's be honest; three minutes is generous. Holding my tongue, I was in visceral discomfort.

Remember, before I could shift the pattern, I had to first identify it (with the help of my husband "you're doing it wrong!"), and then disrupt it (keep my mouth shut). I had to interrupt the pattern to see what arose. What I discovered was that if I accepted an unreciprocated act of generosity, I believed that it was only a matter of time before he would demand something in return, or resent me. Being chronically critical felt much safer than the alternative. This is why disrupting patterns is so vital to truly changing behavior; it provides the opportunity to recognize the root issue.

The feelings, thoughts, and bodily reactions that come to the surface when you interrupt an unhelpful habitual pattern will lead you to its cause. This is critical information if you want to create actual change in your life.

Determined, I continued disrupting the pattern with my husband in the kitchen as best I could. I noticed that anytime my husband did anything kind for me, I felt the knee-jerk urge to criticize him. Then, the unbearably painful hyper-anxiety arose as I bit my tongue for as long as I could.

I began to connect the dots with mechanisms that I'd developed as a child when I learned that kindness often came with strings.

"After all I've done for you, the least you could do is…" was a recurring sentiment, spoken and unspoken, throughout my childhood. No matter how irrational the demand or how much it required of me, I was expected to drop everything and acquiesce. I learned that it was safer to deflect gentleness or generosity in the first place. Was it any wonder that receiving kindness in my closest adult relationship was fraught?

The concept of pattern disruption and how the body and its nervous system carry vital data comes from Somatic Experiencing (SE). This discipline emphasizes seeing what happens or arises physically when you stop a pattern.

SE heals trauma and stress by helping people regulate their nervous system. It was an approach that my mother used to heal her burnout as a therapist and thus, introduced to me. Though I continued to work with Dr. Hirsch throughout my twenties, I still dealt with debilitating anxiety. We had made significant progress; I had developed better relationships, and my sense of self had strengthened. Talk therapy and meditation had done a great deal for me yet had taken me only so far. Despite external markers of success, such as rising through the ranks of well-known tech companies, I still contended with crippling anxiety and self-doubt that manifested physically. I had intense pain in my TMJ, the joint that connects the jawbone to the skull. I developed ulcers and had constant headaches—chronically, recurrently, over a span of ten years. Thus, my mother suggested I try SE therapy, just as she had connected me with my meditation teacher and my psychoanalyst years before.

SE gave me access to a deeper layer of myself, connecting my awareness with my body and nervous system. Through SE, I learned how to emotionally regulate and calm a reactive nervous system. The results were profound. My excruciating, chronic pain dissipated. Living pain-free after years of chronic pain freed me in ways I could hardly imagine before. I married my partner, quit my corporate job, and went on to launch and lead my own successful coaching company. The transformation in my body and life was so astounding that I pursued training to become certified in training others in SE. The modality has become an integral part of the MettaWorks method and this chapter's pillar.

Disrupting a pattern and seeing what it reveals teaches you how to listen to your nervous system. A healthy nervous system moves in a wave, ebbing and flowing as you respond to different situations. Even in a healthy nervous system, you have highs and lows. What makes it healthy is that you are able to ride the wave of emotion, whatever it is, and allow it to pass through.

An unhealthy nervous system is flat or stuck. If it's stuck on "high," it's a sign of anxiety and high sensitivity; stuck on low, it's a sign of being in a depressive state. Each state propels knee-jerk responses that may have little to do with the actual situation at hand.

An emotional reaction out of proportion with the situation points to something historic. Example: Tara's extreme visceral response to the idea of changing our schedule indicated a far deeper concern than the calendar itself.

The body carries wisdom and is foundational to long-lasting change. Disrupting patterns can help you access important information that your body and your nervous system hold. Until you transform at the neurological level and learn to regulate your physical nervous system, unconscious patterns will continue to remain in the driver's seat. For Tara, her deep hidden fear that she didn't have what it takes to be CEO would continue to inform her behavior until we brought it to the surface and started attending to her fear.

As we've moved through this book, you've learned the initial pillars of the MettaWorks method. We've talked through the steps required to cultivate a deeper understanding of yourself: identifying your drivers, cultivating self-awareness, reading the room and implicit feedback, and identifying patterns. Like peeling back the layers of an onion, these are the outermost, papery layers, the ones closest to the surface and ostensibly the easiest to access.

As we work with this pillar, disrupting patterns, we start to brush against the tender inner layers. Though still accessible, it takes more nuanced inner work to understand the information underneath those patterns.

Disrupting patterns teaches you how to pay attention, and listen to your body and your nervous system. Regulating the nervous system is all about building the capacity to manage the ups and downs, so that your system can always return to a healthy ebb and flow. Communication from the body doesn't have to be obvious, like a racing heartbeat, cold sweat, or Tara's sudden tears. It can be a quiet nudge or subtle sensation, often presenting as an emotional response. The key is to listen, gather data, and leverage the information to understand what your body is revealing to you.

Then, pause. Step back and witness. This moment's pause before responding or acting inserts choice into the situation. You can then decide what to do with the information. Rather than "follow your gut," listen to your gut and see what it has to say. Then decide what parts you want to listen to. A critical part of gaining mastery of our inner world is having a space between the body's reaction and our choice as to what to do next.

Through our work together, Tara became clear that the real issue was not about her calendar. She started to trust in the value she had to offer as CEO and became clear about what her role needed to look like in order to be successful. Tara did indeed move her sessions to working hours. She found that this small act gave her the positive feedback she needed to see how taking charge of her calendar was not only ok, it was vital to her stepping into her role as CEO. By creating stronger boundaries, she gained the respect of her people, had more time to think about the bigger picture and make better decisions. The following year, Tara took the company in a new direction and earned a reputation as an industry gamechanger. The company has had its best year yet.

You, too, can learn to pick up on your body's messages and use its guidance in straightforward, practical ways that make a difference for yourself and your people. (Hint: the body is a direct connection to your inner compass.) Listening to and heeding the nervous system strengthens your relationship with yourself, which strengthens your relationships with your team, colleagues, and other stakeholders.

Your exercise this week: select one of the patterns you identified at the end of the last chapter. Interrupt it and notice what happens. Ask yourself:

On a scale of 1 to 10, 1 being entirely appropriate and 10 being outrageously misattuned, how appropriate is my reaction to the situation?

What information is this reaction offering me?

What part of my reaction do I want to listen to?

What part may reflect something from my personal history that I brought with me?

What do I notice when I try to not engage my usual pattern?

Disrupting patterns is vital for you to be in charge of your reactions. It is incredibly powerful once you become accustomed to witnessing your physical response without falling into a knee-jerk reaction. This means becoming comfortable with being uncomfortable. Stand witness to what is revealed. It's not about overriding the pattern; it's stopping to observe the pattern.

Remember to be compassionate with yourself as you disrupt a pattern. It can be easy to beat yourself up. This is especially true as you become familiar with recurrent patterns. You may feel like "I've been here before," and you probably have. Notice how your relationship to the pattern has changed. Remember that this path is not linear; it's a spiral journey. Even if you are stuck in perpetuating the pattern, simply acknowledge: "I am choosing to indulge this pattern right now." By coming from a place of choice, you can then shift things to move toward releasing the old pattern.

By disrupting your patterns, you see what is revealed. Then, and only then, can you begin to understand the resistance beneath it and gain access to the underlying survival mechanisms. Patterns are the output of our resistance. They are the outlet for long-entrenched mechanisms, which are really just older, more embedded patterns, usually learned and incorporated at a tender age. Until you understand what is steering the patterns that keep you off track from your deep desire to show up differently, you will remain stuck in those patterns.

Now it's time to dive into the next layer of this inner journey: embracing the very mechanisms that disrupting your patterns reveals.

CHAPTER 8

Embracing Your Survival Mechanisms

*"Let yourself become that space that welcomes
any experience without judgment."*
—Tsoknyi Rinpoche

"Rachel, they're asking the impossible." Eric was visibly upset. He rubbed his palms against his pant legs; his shoulders raised halfway to his ears. He started clicking a pen in his right hand, nervously tapping it against the desk.

As VP of Engineering at a newly acquired tech company, the demands on Eric and his team had grown exponentially since the merger. He was in the midst of a particularly hairy, cross-functional political situation: the company was changing software platforms, and there was discord around the project's architecture. Leadership was looking to him and his team to work in tandem with other departments and get everyone on the same page.

"We can't do any more than we already are!" he said. "They asked me to spearhead this project… I said, there's no way. It's not happening. We're maxed out. Besides, I'm not familiar with the new platform. I don't know how to do this. How can I take the lead on this project??" He paused for a breath for the first time since our session began and stared at me, a look of pure desperation on his face.

Had Eric and I just started working together, I might have taken his protests at face value. He clearly felt overwhelmed and justified in refusing to participate in the project. Except. His favorite word is "No." Team members come to him with new ideas: No. Proposals on new process improvements: No. Stakeholder requests to add to the roadmap: No. In our work together, we identified this reflexive no as a pattern that limits his ability to influence. It was part of the reason his peers found him so difficult to work with. As we had spent a previous session talking about this very pattern, it felt like a ripe time to disrupt it.

"Let's step back for a moment," I said. "Where's the no coming from?"

"I'm worried about the outrageous workload if I say yes," Eric responded. In his mind, it was an either/or situation. No, he couldn't do it, or yes, he could. As far as he was concerned, there was no option for him to say "yes" with qualifiers; yes, with asking questions; yes, with managing expectations, or asking what the requester would like prioritized as a result of the yes to this project.

Eric had no idea how to create boundaries if he said yes. For him, yes was the equivalent of rolling over and becoming a doormat. Saying no was the easier route.

"I have no time, Rachel; I'm putting in extra hours as it is. My partner is ready to kill me; I show up late for dinner. I cancel plans last minute. It's not good!" Eric continued to protest. "And my team is working as hard as I am, if not harder. I'm afraid they're gonna burn out."

He felt like he didn't know how to manage what little time the team had. And so, everything was "no." Eric, appropriately, didn't want to take on more. That instinct was spot on. Creating clear lines in the sand was essential for his role and for keeping his team from getting swamped.

His intention was correct. He wanted to protect his team's time, energy, and focus; however, his "no" left no room for conversation. That was the issue, and it had real ramifications. Eric alienated stakeholders, and as a result, people undermined him. The executive team had even passed him over for a recent promotion. No one wanted to work with him.

It was essential for Eric to not only create boundaries and set expectations but to proactively communicate those boundaries and expectations to stakeholders. Instead of his automatic, knee-jerk no, he needed to learn how to say, "Yes… And what, then, do you want to fall off the list?"

Just changing his verbiage was a step in the right direction, but for change to take hold in the long-term, Eric needed to do more inner work first. He needed to learn and incorporate the next pillar of the MettaWorks method, identifying and acknowledging the survival mechanism driving his habitual no: the belief that he would inevitably get steamrolled the moment he said yes.

Before we could touch the underlying mechanism, pattern identification was a necessary first step, as you learned a couple of chapters ago. It allows us to see when we're recreating and repeating an unhelpful behavior. Patterns hide what we don't want to look at. Identifying the survival mechanism that underlies the pattern allows us to solve the correct problem. If we only shift the behavioral pattern itself (saying no), the change won't last. The survival mechanism will remain in the driver's seat and find another outlet.

Once we disrupt the pattern, we uncover the survival mechanism: what we believe. Survival mechanisms are belief systems that no longer work for us. They are behavioral structures we didn't even realize were in charge. As you'll recall from the last chapter, one way to tell if a pattern is rooted in a survival mechanism is simple: disrupt it and see what happens. Eric would have to disrupt the pattern of his no, in order to reveal and ultimately acknowledge the mechanism driving his habitual behavior. But we weren't there yet.

"What do you feel, Eric, when I suggest saying yes with a qualifier instead of no?" I asked.

Eric was already shaking his head. "No, Rachel. Impossible. NO WAY."

"Check in for a moment: what is your immediate reaction at the thought of saying yes?" I responded.

"I don't see how that would solve anything. It just creates more work for me. It makes me really nervous," Eric said.

Earlier in Eric's career, as an individual contributor, saying no allowed him to manage his time better and prevented him from taking on too much, overpromising, and falling short of delivering. It benefited him to say no. However, the intensity of his feelings suggested that the mechanism was older than that. "What are you worried would happen if you said yes?" I said.

Eric rubbed his hand over his mouth, deep in thought. "No good... Been there, done that. If I say yes, then I become a doormat and give everything away. If I say yes, I have no leverage."

If/then statements are a great sign of a survival mechanism at work. This particular one is a conversation I've had many times with clients. As we talked, Eric realized this had been a pattern throughout his life. "It's like *If You Give a Mouse a Cookie*..." Familiar with the children's book, I grinned and nodded, urging him to say more.

"My partner and I refer to that book all the time.... You remember the story: if you give a mouse a cookie, he'll ask for a glass of milk. And then a napkin. A nap. And pretty soon the mouse has moved in and is eating you out of house and home. We both have similar patterns with our families, so it's become a kind of code word and a running joke in our household."

"I can see how saying *No* would feel safer," I said. "Like you have more control over the outcome. And, we've stumbled on something important here: what is *driving* your automatic *No*. It's a pattern, a belief, a *survival mechanism*." Saying yes, for Eric, was a slippery slope, as he learned when he was growing up. Now, as an adult, he applied his childhood experience, fearing forfeiting his own needs and the needs of his team. Is it any wonder that his favorite word was no?

EMBRACING YOUR SURVIVAL MECHANISMS

It's akin to my experience, disrupting the pattern of criticizing my husband in the kitchen. In the (maybe) three minutes I kept my mouth shut and didn't criticize him, I was in visceral discomfort. It was painful and nearly impossible. However, once I was able to disrupt the pattern and hang out in that discomfort, it became apparent that I felt a deep vulnerability around receiving something without immediately reciprocating. I thought I had to manage the situation as anxiety flooded my system. Was my husband going to criticize me? Was he going to hang it over my head later that I didn't do for him when he did for me? Was he keeping a tally of all the things he's done for me that I haven't done for him?

The belief I developed as a child was that receiving comes at a cost. When I was growing up, we had very little money. My parents collectively made less than $30,000 a year, working 12 hours a day. I got exactly one new outfit a year for the first day of school. The rest of my clothes were hand-me-downs that my mom's best friend brought over in a garbage bag, which was a high point that I still think fondly of. It felt like going shopping!

The only reason we were able to scrape by was due to the generosity of my incredibly wealthy aunt. She not only paid for my mother's schooling to get her Ph.D. but also covered our rent while she did. We were very fortunate to be the recipients of her sponsorship. Without her continued support, it's not hyperbolic to say we would have lost our home. My mom would have had to drop out of school. My parents would have had to find different work. The trajectory of our lives would have changed completely.

My family was under constant financial pressure, and it was of dire importance that we stay in the good graces of my aunt. My aunt and her family observed Shabbat religiously, so part of maintaining the relationship meant attending Shabbat dinner at her home every other Friday night.

Picture this: we're a family barely getting by, walking into a $5 million (in the 1990s, so you can imagine what it would be worth now), two-level penthouse apartment with marble floors, terraces and an exclusive elevator and doorman for their floor. We would take drinks and appetizers in the living room in front of the marble fireplace, and then dinner was served to us in the formal dining room by live-in staff.

As the only child at the time, and focal point at the table, participating in adult conversations in this rarified, foreign environment, I felt like I had to show up and be perfect. I felt I always had to say and do the right things, speak intelligently, but not too much. I had to be flawless, because, in my young mind, if I weren't, we'd lose my aunt's assistance.

The belief that arose from that fear and drove me was this: if I were not hyper-vigilant and managing all the relationships and interactions in the room, the world would fall apart, and we'd lose what little we had. I could not drop my high alertness and consummate performance for a solitary moment. In my young mind, the consequences were a matter of life and death. I was four. This constant dynamic continued until I was twelve.

When you hear this, you might think, "Of course that little girl couldn't be in control of her aunt's generosity." That is a rational, adult conclusion. Survival mechanisms and patterns are not born of rational interpretations, but of potent emotional imprints and subtle or explicit messages we receive as very small children. To me, our very survival depended upon me to make sure that everyone was okay, so that we did not jeopardize my aunt's sponsorship.

Hence my survival mechanism: being hyper-vigilant about the needs of all others in the room, ensuring everyone got what they wanted, what they needed, in order to be ok. I became highly skilled at reading a room, understanding what's going on for other people, and meeting their needs. These abilities make me a very skilled coach (my superpower) while also causing me to feel responsible for directly managing any discord or conflict in the room (my kryptonite).

I want to be in charge of how this mechanism expresses itself in my work and life. *I* want to decide when I want to attend to the needs of others. *I* want to decide when I need to be managing the dynamics in a room. The pieces I don't so much want to keep? The part that causes me to panic if everybody is not okay; the belief embedded in my psyche that generosity is tenuous and conditional, and the giver can yank the gift back at any time.

Fast forward to being in the kitchen with my husband. The stakes are so much lower than they felt when I was four. I am in a loving relationship. I help contribute to our family's well-being. I know I am in charge of my survival and not beholden to an elder benefactress. The only reason I was able to see this clearly was because I had consistently and persistently disrupted the pattern of criticism which felt so necessary to my ok-ness.

Patterns cover the pieces that we long ago decided we would never look at. For me, my pattern was hiding my survival mechanism around receiving. The story I'd learned was that no kindness came without strings, so I pushed away any kind act with my criticism. It was safer and less stressful to rebuff the gift in the first place. For Eric, it was that saying yes meant giving away your autonomy. It was safer and less stressful to say no. Always.

"I have the utmost respect for our survival mechanisms," I said to Eric. "Before we look at shifting yours or giving it a new job, we need to celebrate it. It must be doing some good work, given that it has gotten you this far. How has it protected you, benefited you, worked for you up until now?"

Our survival mechanisms are just that: mechanisms that helped us survive at a critical moment in our lives. They are deeply entrenched because they protected us at a more vulnerable time. We created these systems at a very young age when we could not survive without the food, water, and love provided by the adults in our lives. Thus, we created survival tactics to get those things and stay alive. As such, they have deep roots intertwined with our very sense of safety. Hence, the terror when we disrupt them.

As adults, many of those survival mechanisms become our super-powers and our kryptonite. For Eric, his superpower is having firm and clear boundaries; his kryptonite is the all-or-nothing mindset that creates artificial limitations in his ability to partner with his peers.

"Having that survival mechanism protected me—my time, my team's time," he reflected. "It's allowed me to be as productive as I've been. It's gotten me to where I am today." Now, it was time for Eric to be more discerning about this survival mechanism's influence in his life. We needed to shine a light on the fact that the belief that a yes is dangerous isn't always accurate.

"How on a scale of 1-10, 1 being not true at all and 10 being entirely true, is it that you have to give it all away if you say yes? That it's an all-or-nothing proposition?" I asked.

Eric tilted his head thoughtfully. "Cognitively, I know it isn't true. But emotionally? It feels completely true, like a 10. Saying yes feels like I will completely lose control of the situation."

"Creating boundaries is of real service..." I responded. "Your no isn't *wrong*. But when is it not helpful?"

"Well, it kept me from getting my most recent promotion. No one likes that I say no all the time," Eric said.

"We need to provide updated information to your survival mechanism so that you can embrace it without it being your kryptonite. Your no can be used for good," I said.

So often, we have a love-hate relationship with our survival mechanisms. Once we've identified one, we want to "get rid of it." Or trample over it. If Eric had simply altered the behavior pattern at a surface level and mixed in some "yeses" with his "noes," the change wouldn't last. People wouldn't buy it because he didn't. If I'd gritted my teeth and forced myself to say "thank you" whenever anyone offered a kind act, the criticism would simply leave my mouth after my "thank you." Unfortunately, these behaviors are only superficial solutions. This is called overriding the survival mechanism, and if we do that, we are in for a world of trouble. Our old survival mechanisms will find some other way to express themselves. They will leak out in ways over which we have absolutely no control.

Instead, you need to have compassion and celebrate your survival mechanisms. Really. You need to throw them a party! They've done incredible work for you. They've kept you alive and helped you get where you are today.

What is key here is not dismissing, judging, or suppressing the survival mechanism. You don't want to throw them out. The gentler and more compassionate you are with your survival mechanisms (and yourself), the more likely you will change the patterns that no longer work for you.

Tsoknyi Rinpoche, a Nepalese Tibetan Buddhist teacher, talks about how simply being with your "beautiful monsters," i.e., your difficult emotions and unhelpful patterns, with a non-judgmental, compassionate, embodied awareness, allows your beautiful monsters to open and transform naturally. This same approach is effective with your survival mechanisms: witness them. Be with them. In the context of this conversation, your survival mechanisms are *your* beautiful monsters. They are beautiful because they've taken care of you. They've kept you safe. Or rather: they did, once upon a time. Often, when you were younger, a lot younger.

The next step is to bring the survival mechanisms to the table and have a thoughtful conversation with them in a way you haven't before, when they were running the show. It's no longer appropriate for them to run the show, but they don't have to leave. This decision is not an either-or, between letting the mechanisms be in charge or evicting them from your life.

Yes, you have to do the deep inner work to shift these old patterns, but that doesn't mean you burn it all down. If you try to go through this process quickly, you'll get the rubber band effect. Pull a rubber band rapidly to its limits, then release it. It bounces right back to the size it was when you started, maybe even smaller. However, you can gradually stretch the rubber band, putting it over a small object, then a larger one, then an even larger one. In that case, the rubber band will eventually hold its elongated shape and won't snap back.

At MettaWorks, we use a similar approach when working with your survival mechanisms. This process involves gently and gradually updating information with the survival mechanism. In uncovering my survival mechanism around receiving, it felt empowering for me to recognize my own deeply learned behavior and beliefs. I realized that all I needed to do was update the file. It was a matter of educating that little girl that she is now the adult in the room: we have a roof over our heads, everything's going to be okay.

When Eric learned to embrace his survival mechanism, what was once a knee-jerk reaction became a superpower. His "no" was less automatic and more thoughtful; his yes brought qualifiers and questions when necessary. As a result, his "no" started to be respected. His team felt protected. It also helped him create boundaries in his life for a better work-life balance. Once he embraced his powerful survival mechanism and stayed in the driver's seat himself, he learned that he could apply his superpower in a variety of situations.

Through Eric's work on his own survival mechanisms, his relationships at the peer level greatly improved. This is yet another example of how the inner work you do directly impacts your success as a leader. As a leader, you've heard me say, again and again, that your relationships are your deliverables. This idea is fundamental to your success as a leader at the highest echelons. Before my clients understand this, they stay mired in managing people, executing, and spinning their wheels. Until you focus on your relationships as your deliverables, you'll always be solving the wrong problem. The first step in focusing on those relationships is cultivating your relationship with yourself. This requires doing the inner work, each pillar of the MettaWorks method I've described so far. These are ideas that bear repeating because they take some repetition to truly sink in and shift you at the deepest levels.

When you understand your survival mechanisms and embrace them for how they have served you, you not only understand what you can let go of, you also become clear as to how they can continue to serve you.

Now, it's your turn. Take a closer look at a pattern you disrupted at the end of the last chapter.

What is the survival mechanism, the deeply entrenched story behind that pattern?

How did that mechanism serve you in the past?

When did you first learn that survival mechanism?

Thank your survival mechanism for its hard work. Throw it a party! You can't touch a pattern until you start celebrating and honoring your survival mechanisms behind it. Embrace your survival mechanisms; sit and be with your "beautiful monsters" without judging or rejecting them.

This is a crucial step because when you identify your survival mechanisms and have the courage to start to shift them, resistance shows up. Resistance can stop you in your tracks if you don't understand how to meet it and move through it. That is where we head next.

CHAPTER 9

Understanding Your Resistance

"Out of resistance comes strength."
—Napoleon Hill

"I don't know what to do," Tara groaned, rolling her eyes. Where once Tara wanted nothing more than to "get out of here" (remember from the chapter on disrupting patterns), she and I had been making really good progress together. She had been embracing her survival mechanisms, gaining clarity on when they served her and when they were getting in her way. She had taken charge of her calendar and had more time for big-picture thinking. She was stepping self-assuredly into her role as CEO.

As often happens when you run a company, an issue arose that Tara needed to address. The product team made a serious mistake that negatively impacted specific high-profile clients. As a result, it was Tara's responsibility to tend to those client relationships. Tara was procrastinating as the deadline of having to resolve the situation kept getting closer and closer. Tara was stuck, immobilized, and confused.

These were indicators to me that Tara had entered a place of resistance. Resistance arises when we are starting to shift a deeply entrenched survival mechanism. It is the smoke and mirrors that will distract you from facing and moving through your fear of getting to the other side, of being the change you want to make. Great indicators of resistance are procrastination, defensiveness, collapse, immobilization, and avoidance, to name a few.

Resistance is your survival mechanism's last-ditch effort to prevent you from changing.

"Let's step back for a minute. What has shifted since we started working together?" I asked.

"I've been asserting my voice, gaining clarity on my role. I am more comfortable being in charge and acting as the decision-maker. That's why it was so important to take back my calendar, so I was in charge of my time."

"There is so much to celebrate! Look how far you've come.. So, what's different with this scenario? What is giving you pause in dealing with the impacted clients?"

"There isn't a difference. That's just it, Rachel. I know what I need to do. I need to tell the client what we are and are not responsible for and what we can and cannot do—" Tara's voice sounded stronger and clearer even as she spoke the words. "And yet when it comes time to send an email or pick up the phone, I'm suddenly at a loss for words. Gah, what is wrong with me?" Tara put her face in her hands.

"There's nothing wrong with you," I reassured Tara. "Actually, it's a sign of something going really right. This is resistance showing up. A mentor of mine describes resistance as the thing that wraps itself around the fear—so you don't have to look at the fear itself."

"So... this is why I've been going around in circles for weeks?" asked Tara.

"It can feel discouraging, but it's actually a really good sign. It means that you are continuing to challenge your old survival mechanisms. You are continuing to disrupt patterns and create new ones. When resistance shows up, it means you are on the right path! You're not regressing. You've changed a lot. This immobility is an opportunity to notice and ask, *"What's happening here?"*

"When resistance shows up, as it is for you right now," I continued, "it shows that you've started to shift a survival mechanism that has kept you from truly embodying the role of decision maker as CEO. Your resistance is pulling out all the stops in an effort to return you to your old definition of safety. That's why you've felt so confused, even though you know exactly what to do. You are challenging the sentry guarding the castle, Tara, and that is a really good thing, *not* something to beat yourself up over."

Tara nodded, pensive. "So, the confusion and feeling immobilized by the whole thing... these were all a distraction, so I don't look at my fear of the thing we've been working on this whole time? Being in charge, being the decision maker..."

I nodded. "You got it."

"I still feel a little discouraged," Tara admitted. "But I get what you're saying."

"If we kick ourselves for having resistance in the first place, we're just as stuck. By acknowledging it without judgment, we can take the next step. The work doesn't end there, however."

"Ugh, does it ever?" Tara sighed.

I laughed commiseratingly. "Well, no and yes... There are always places we can go deeper and improve more. But every time we do this work, we shift our perspective. Every time, we're starting from a better place. The process gets faster and easier."

Resistance means you're successfully challenging a survival mechanism that you want to change your relationship to. Resistance will show up when you're doing this deeper work. In order to alter the unhelpful pattern that the survival mechanism creates in your life, you need to move through the resistance. You need to continue with the new helpful behavior; otherwise, the pattern remains entrenched.

Understanding and hanging out in the resistance is profoundly important and powerful. It demands a slow, careful pace. With resistance, the slower you go, the faster you change. Resistance is slippery and incredibly smart. It will always have great reasons why something won't work. It will always provide a compelling and powerful aversion to anything new you are trying that challenges the status quo.

"I just need to…" is another great indicator of resistance. In an earlier chapter, I referenced this phrase as an indicator of a pattern. If examined closely, often this can be an indicator of a resistance pattern. The "just" indicates that it hasn't happened yet and is a signal to pause and ask, "What is getting in the way of me doing so?" Another indicator of resistance is when you keep repeating the same behavior over and over again despite wanting to do it differently. Confusion or immobility where we're normally competent is an additional sign that resistance is in the room. Other good indicators of resistance include collapse, finger-pointing, increased criticism, defensiveness, and minimizing.

When encountering resistance, standard coaching will ask questions such as: What's important to you? What's your goal? What are the roadblocks? What's getting in the way? This beginning is vital to change. However, sustainable change only comes by going deeper than the cognitive level of creating and sticking with a goal. The MettaWorks method goes much deeper and explores the why behind the resistance. This deeper approach helps us to understand what is keeping us from meeting our goals on a visceral level. By looking beyond the behavior to its root, we start to understand that factors such as our early history, systems of oppression, and our storyline live in our nervous system. These experiences have created survival mechanisms that can only shift if they are first identified and attended to. Understanding the resistance or roadblock will help us solve the right problem.

One of the ways we began to attend to Tara's resistance was by creating a mantra that she would repeat when she noticed that she was confused or paralyzed. In those moments, she was to ask herself, "What am I avoiding responsibility for here?" By recognizing the resistance and not buying the story of her confusion, she was then able to ask a deeper question. She was able to attend to the fear under the resistance and address the root of the issue, which was her feeling that she was unworthy as a CEO.

Resistance showed up for me several years ago when I was ready to take my business to the next level of growth. I knew I needed to be more visible and consistent with my marketing. I wanted my blog to convey the depth and nuance of the work that MettaWorks does with our clients. I hired a copywriter to help make it a reality. It was no small undertaking. I put in hours of time and effort to develop the content, review it, and approve it. All I needed to do was hit "send." And yet: I couldn't do it.

Every time I went to send the first blog article out, I would suddenly feel like there were other more important things to attend to. I would feel tired. I would have thought "it's not quite ready yet." I didn't recognize it as resistance right away. I literally did not know what was going on. Why couldn't I hit send? This is precisely how sneaky and slippery resistance is.

Three sessions in a row, my business coach asked, "So, how are the blogs going?"

I had nothing to report. "I just can't get it together to do it," I said, finally.

This experience with my business brought to the surface something I didn't realize was profoundly deep: a belief that it's not okay for me to be seen. The story went, if I were truly seen, I would be criticized. I wasn't fully aware of how deep and powerful this belief was for me until my resistance to publishing my blog gave me a doorway into accessing it. Sharing those articles with the world was a manifestation of me using my voice and me sharing my perspective, even if that perspective wasn't shared by everybody else.

It took me a year to send that first article. Now, a new blog article is shared with my community twice a month, consistently and easily. None of this would have been possible without first seeing and acknowledging my resistance.

Resistance can be a powerful gift, revealing deeper parts of yourself that no longer serve you. It is normal to encounter resistance when you engage a survival mechanism and begin to shift it. In fact, you should assume and expect that resistance will show up when you engage your survival mechanism. It means you are on the right path, going in the right direction, and doing the right work.

Once she started using it regularly, Tara's mantra became a powerful tool. Whenever she encountered confusion that kept her from taking action, it became a red flag, a reminder that it was time to ask herself the question: "What am I avoiding responsibility for here?"

This simple practice led Tara to swifter and more certain decisions and actions. The question had an instant clarifying effect, like a hot knife through butter: dispelling the confusion and immobility and allowing her to disrupt these old patterns. As we touched on when you first met Tara, the external results of her inner work were prodigious: she took the company in a new direction to have its best year yet, becoming known as an industry gamechanger.

Resistance can seem insurmountable when it shows up. The point is to prepare for the resistance. Expect and acknowledge it. Once you do, get curious about the resistance and stay with it. Sit in the resistance, like a child in the mud. Get dirty, explore, and see what unfolds. It becomes possible to move through it when (and only when) you recognize it, name it and get curious about what is hiding underneath it.

"Resistance is arising to be liberated," says one of my mentors when movement forward continues to feel impossible. It's only when we start to see, "Oh... this is resistance. This is what's creating difficulty for me," that things actually start to shift. That's why it's not about changing your resistance, it's about understanding your resistance that's so important. Resistance is an indicator of a survival mechanism in hiding. As you learned in the last chapter, the survival mechanism is the belief system that needs to be updated, like a program. Understanding resistance takes time and a lot of deep work, and once you do, you discover a deeper layer of information about your inner world.

As I struggled to launch my blog and increase my visibility, I had to become okay with the idea that this is who I am, not what everybody else might want from me. My resistance in the course of my work gave me a new frontier for dealing with my survival mechanisms.

Now it's your turn:

Notice the indicators of resistance, in yourself.

Where is resistance getting in the way of you doing something you want to do?

How is resistance slowing your progress? For yourself as an individual or your team?

Simply becoming aware of your resistance (remember the chapter on cultivating awareness) will allow you to recognize it, name it and get curious about what hides underneath it.

CHAPTER 10

Survival Mechanisms Become Your Superpowers

"The things that make us different, those are our superpowers."
—Lena Waithe

"How can I get anything done and accomplish our goals now that we've been acquired?"

Oscar, Chief Information Officer of a recently acquired high-growth tech company, was now smack in the middle of an organization many times bigger than the one he'd led. Recently, he felt like his hands were often tied in strategic decision-making. Oscar's frustration was legitimate; he couldn't wield the same type of influence as he had when he was in the topmost ranks of the company. He no longer had final input on the company roadmap.

"I get your frustration. Let's step back and look at the big picture for a minute. What do you want long-term?" I asked. At such a pivotal moment in his career it was vital that he identify his drivers, come back to his anchor, and remember his "why" (the first pillar of the MettaWorks method).

"To be CEO," Oscar answered definitively. It was an aspiration he'd had for a long time. "CEO of a larger company than my old one. Pre-merger, I mean. An enterprise a bit like this one, actually…" He paused thoughtfully.

I sensed Oscar's energy shift, as his thoughts went from frustration to possibility. He was beginning to see an opportunity where he'd only seen a challenge before.

Remember the chapter on identifying drivers and the importance of tuning into one's aspirations. When we do so, we often get a perspective that takes us out of the weeds and toward a bigger vision. Sometimes our aspirations and drivers shift, expand or even get clearer as we continue to do this inner work. This is another reason why it is important that we return to them periodically.

Seeing how quickly Oscar was able to let go of his frustration reminded me of how far he'd come. "Remember when we first started working together?"

"I do." Oscar's eyes twinkled. Oscar had been a bullish leader. Aggressive in achieving company goals, he steamrolled anyone or anything that got in his way. He had an explosive temper and consistently raised his voice. His belligerence was part of what made his company successful and led to it becoming acquired. This behavior was also why he'd been nominated for coaching.

"Can we take a moment to celebrate the progress we've made? A year ago you still would have been ranting about the situation at work for at least three more sessions." I smiled.

"True that," Oscar said, laughing. In our work together, Oscar was no longer bulldozing those around him to get things done. Now that he had tools to effectively get his point across without offending people, it was time to help him cultivate a more sophisticated set of communication skills.

"I can't push my agenda like I used to," he mused aloud. "I've had to be more creative…"

"Right. You've come a long way, and learned how to influence rather than—"

"Yell until everyone was on board, or pretended to be?" Oscar interjected.

I smiled and nodded. "You're in a different place now," I said.

In our work together, we had discovered that beneath his explosiveness was a fear of losing control and the perceived safety of being in control. Previously, to maintain control, Oscar would micromanage his team, incessantly and aggressively. His survival mechanism manifested as yelling in order to be heard and heeded by others. This behavior rewarded him with a sense of control. The problem was, his explosive behavior eroded relationships. As I've said before (and will say again): your success as an executive is in your relationships. Your people are your deliverables. Yes, Oscar got things done, but at a high cost. This behavior is what had limited Oscar's growth as a leader.

Survival mechanisms are implicit assumptions you make that are especially entrenched because they are often formed during childhood. On a deep level, you believe your very survival depends on them. As you learned previously, resistance is that last-ditch effort of your subconscious to hide your survival mechanisms. When you dig deeper, these mechanisms often reveal themselves as unquestioned "if/then" statements. Oscar's survival mechanism manifested as: "If I'm not in control, I'll die." The way that he learned to be in control was by raising his voice and strongly asserting his opinion. Spoken aloud, it's clear that Oscar's underlying "if/then" statement couldn't possibly be true. This is how survival mechanisms work. They make absolute statements that helped us survive at an earlier time, that no longer serve us.

In order to help shift a survival mechanism, to reiterate what we talked about in the last chapter, you need to first celebrate it and then give it updated information. The survival mechanism was born of experiences from another time. As a result, it is driving you to respond to your current environment in ways that are no longer skillful. You must help the survival mechanism see that your circumstances have changed. It is important to work with your survival mechanism, versus get rid of it. It simply needs a new job.

Every survival mechanism holds within it important wisdom. This is the hidden superpower. In order to access it, you need to take the time to point your mechanism toward a new constructive purpose, versus your previous (unconscious) harmful behaviors.

For Oscar, in order to progress, we needed to honor his survival mechanism and give it a different job. We needed to harness it as a superpower. What was the wisdom within Oscar's loud communication style? He was willing and able to get things done, no matter the cost, no matter the work. Pre-acquisition, Oscar's loud communication style had already started to shift dramatically as a result of our work. With that being said, he still led with a strong dictatorial style. His former position in the organization and his presence allowed him to make decisions quickly and effectively across the organization.

The acquisition triggered Oscar's survival mechanism, challenging his sense of control and safety. All of a sudden, he felt like he had no power. The new structure didn't allow him to get things done in the way that he had been able to before. He'd always been able to push things through. His leadership by force wasn't working anymore because post-acquisition the organization was much more complex and bureaucratic. The leadership structure was in flux. Oscar's role had changed. Much to his disappointment, he was not a final decision maker anymore.

"What would happen, if you reframed your current situation?" I said. "What if you leveraged the role you're in now to develop the skills you'll need as CEO—while getting paid to do it?"

Oscar's ears pricked up. We talked through what it takes to be a successful CEO, and the skills that he still required in order to do so. A significant skill set he lacked was advocating for his ideas in subtle, less visible ways and thus, growing his influence. He didn't have to be loud; he could have the same impact without giving orders.

When he saw the opportunity to cultivate a new skill set that would make him a successful CEO, he realized he had more power in his current role than he was giving himself credit for.

When you nurture a new pattern of behavior, like turning a survival mechanism into a superpower, it opens up a whole world of possibilities. You have no idea what was possible previously. You couldn't; you were unaware. When Oscar was stuck in a pattern of directing, rather than influencing and guiding as a leader, there was no way he could get from there to CEO. When you educate the survival mechanism and become in charge of it, you are able to shift its purpose. It can become one of your greatest superpowers. Oscar shifted his default behavior of dictating, to leading through others.

The wisdom buried in Oscar's survival mechanism, the unwavering belief that he could get anything done no matter the cost, meant that he didn't care how it got done. In other words, he was not attached to how things got done; therefore, he was really open to different possibilities. In the past, this is what gave him sharp elbows, because he didn't care if getting things done meant destroying relationships in the process. As he embraced the idea that his relationships make or break his success as a leader, and learned to work *with* instead of against his survival mechanism, he could leverage this wisdom for good.

It's really important to honor the wisdom of the survival mechanism. For Tara, the survival mechanism her resistance tried to hide was a deep ingrained sense of responsibility. Her old belief system held that her survival depended on her personal responsibility. Hence why she was driven to take more on her calendar than she could; hence why she stalled when resolving the client issue. By honoring and mining the wisdom of her mechanism, the question "What am I not taking responsibility for?" became a powerful tool for cutting through the resistance and patterning to her taking decisive action. It was using her mechanism toward her success, versus letting it halt her progress.

For Oscar, his deep commitment to getting things done no matter what could be converted into a simple question: "Ok, what needs to get done here?" His openness to how, his superpower, meant that he couldn't be stopped just because the new structure doesn't allow for his old ways. He was free to ask, "So what is the new way? What is the way to be successful in this new organizational structure?" Again, it didn't matter how things were executed, as long as they got done.

Since Oscar wasn't attached to how things got done, this allowed him to let go of his ego and experiment. He could "read the tea leaves" of his environment and arrive at: what's a better way to do this? It wasn't just about adapting to the culture of the company; he actually upleveled himself as a leader as a result.

He wielded his influence in a more subtle, nuanced way. He focused his considerable influence on acquiring the skills he would need as CEO. The impact was unmistakable. Colleagues who'd known Oscar for years spotted the difference. He took more time to listen to others' ideas, waiting to provide his own insights when asked. He used open-ended questions, facilitated thoughtful conversations, provided powerful insights, and became a valued sounding board to leaders across the new organization.

People throughout the company started quoting Oscar's ideas. They sought him out for advice. Recently, a colleague advocated for Oscar's department to get more headcount without him even being in the room, during a tight budget season, no less. If that doesn't scream influence, I don't know what does! Oscar knew his ideas were moving the company in a productive direction as he built the skills that would win him the role of CEO of a much larger organization.

Turning survival mechanisms into superpowers requires giving them a new job. Just like Oscar, before you can do that, you have to embrace them. You must understand how the survival mechanism has been serving you. Only then can you solve the real issue or challenge at hand. Until then, you're just unconsciously acting out patterns, much like Oscar yelling to get things done.

I learned this firsthand with one of my survival mechanisms: "Save me."

Remember the story I shared earlier of being dependent on my wealthy aunt's generosity for my family's survival? That experience translated into a belief system that it's not okay to be independent: "If I'm independent or self-sufficient, if I don't need saving or rescuing, then I will lose my benefactor's support (and die)." This statement sounds really crazy when you say it out loud. That illogic is the nature of survival mechanisms. They are irrational, unconscious assumptions that we make early on. They bury themselves deep and drive our behavior until we acknowledge them. Only in acknowledging them can we integrate them and give them new purpose.

Any difficult or challenging situation triggered my fear of independence. "I can't navigate this alone." In the moment where I encountered a roadblock or impasse, I would collapse. I would remain collapsed until one of the people closest to me stepped in and saved me. The work for me has been about being able to be independent and thrive in the face of challenges and difficulties.

Through years of my own personal work and taking myself through the MettaWorks methodology, I discovered my superpower that emerged from this survival mechanism. My superpower is that I know when to ask for help, and do so easily. I believe support is always available to me. When faced with a challenge, my first go-to step is to leverage the help of an expert. This means that I have become a terrific delegator. This superpower has allowed me to make quick decisions in my business and hire the right people to execute on important tasks. This ability to know how and when to ask for help has taken my business from a solo operation to a company with a robust, high-functioning team.

By turning your survival mechanisms into superpowers, you take a formerly unconscious energetic pattern and shift it in a way that actually propels you forward, rather than keeping you stuck on repeat. You don't need to surgically remove your issues. In fact, doing so would be a terrible idea. Your survival mechanisms carry a great deal of wisdom and power.

Now, it's your turn.

What mechanism did you identify in the chapter on embracing survival mechanisms, or what triggers have floated to the surface while reading this chapter?

How has your survival mechanism helped you? How has it taken care of you?

What aspects of your survival mechanism no longer serve you?

From this, what underlying wisdom does your survival mechanism bring that you would like to carry forward?

The clearer you are on how a survival mechanism has taken care of you, the more you celebrate it, the more powerful your change in behavior will be. The more solid you are in the wisdom and the gift of your survival mechanism the more powerfully you will be able to leverage your superpowers. The easier your unhelpful behaviors and belief systems will melt away. This is particularly true as you hold yourself accountable, as you will see in the next chapter.

CHAPTER 11

Cultivating Compassionate Accountability

"Love and compassion are necessities, not luxuries.
Without them, humanity cannot survive."
—The Dalai Lama

"I don't know where to begin."

Newly hired on as VP of User Experience, Aliyah had been charged with building a team from the ground up. However, instead of developing the team strategy and working with HR to start recruiting the team, she was immobilized. She was easily distracted and was constantly getting pulled into the weeds of day-to-day details. As you will remember from the chapter on pattern identification, this is a theme she shares in common with Jonas.

Jonas' resistance manifested in doing. He was getting up at midnight to troubleshoot the server because it was easier than dealing with interpersonal relationships. Aliyah's resistance manifested differently and showed up (like Tara's) as confusion.

"I don't know what my vision is for the team," she said. "How am I supposed to create something when I am not yet clear on it myself?"

For several of our sessions, the issue remained the same. Aliyah was trying to develop a strategy. She kept changing her mind and starting the process over. In the meantime, she had no team and was failing to make any strides in hiring. Her experience in building teams was not the issue. Aliyah had built multiple teams, and more than once from the ground up. She had done this before, so what was the problem?

107

When resistance rears up, we often don't immediately identify it as such. As we discussed before, it's the thing that wraps around the fear, disguising it. So resistance is not always immediately apparent. It is an indicator light on the dashboard, informing you that an old pattern is ready to be liberated. In other words, congrats! The work you've been doing is paying off. This is why it can be helpful to have a coach who can reflect back places that are hard to see for ourselves. After our third session retreading the same ground, I asked Aliyah point-blank:

"So. What is going on? You *know* how to do this."

"Sure, I know, Rachel, but…" she looked up at me, shaking her head.

It's not like Aliyah consciously told herself, "I'm scared to build a team at this level; no one's ever built a team like this one. It's easier to get immersed in the weeds of operations and forget everything I know about setting a vision for the team." Instead, she felt sincerely and totally confused.

"Okay. So what happens when I say, let's just make a strategy up and see what happens? What's your immediate reaction?"

"Oh, it's not good enough," Aliyah said with certainty. "No, not good enough."

"Hmm. We know that voice…" I said.

Aliyah looked up at me with a glint of clarity and humor in her eyes that I hadn't seen in weeks. We'd been working together through the pillars of the MettaWorks method long enough for her to recognize one of the beliefs underlying her recurrent patterns. "Yeah, right. 'It's never good enough.' That's where I'm stuck, Rachel."

"Okay, great. So let's talk about that: How true is it? That if you draft a vision, it's not going to be good enough?"

"Riiiight…" The light was dawning as Aliyah spoke. "It can't be true… yet. There's no way to know if it's good enough until I put something out there. I just need something for the leadership team to react to. We have no idea what we want until we have some ideas on the table. This kind of team has never been built before at my company. And yet, every time I think about going to the computer to spend my time on the strategy, I just—" Aliyah's pitch lilted back up to where it was at the start of the session. "Something happens. I feel baffled about where to start."

"Now that you have clarity that 'my strategy isn't good enough' isn't true," I said, "It's time to look at this as a survival mechanism that is no longer appropriate. So, what age is the voice saying 'not good enough'?"

"Thirteen," she answered quickly, then looked at me with surprise. "How did I know that?" Then she smiled. She had been working with me long enough to trust the information that arose from her inner world.

"Interesting. Can you see the 13-year-old?"

"Yeah, I have a sense of her, actually." Aliyah recognized that the 13-year-old is the voice that is constantly shouting, "It's not good enough. It's not gonna be good enough. What do you think you're doing?"

"Okay. So how has this 13-year-old been taking really good care of you?" I started taking her through the pillar, embracing your survival mechanism.

"Well," Aliyah thought for a moment. "I mean, because nothing is ever good enough, I've always strived to do better, constantly trying to improve. I deliver, I keep getting promoted..."

"Yes, that makes so much sense. Your 13-year-old self is part of why you keep being given more responsibility. So we don't want to tell her to get lost."

Aliyah nodded. "Yeah. I don't want to lower my standards."

"Exactly," I said. "She just needs to know the appropriate time to participate. What if you told her that she could take a five-minute break and come back when it was time to evaluate and improve the strategy."

"Mm-hmm. Yeah. She can sit in the same room with me, in the kitchen hanging out making a grilled cheese sandwich, while I just do what needs to get done." As Aliyah said this out loud, I could feel her entire nervous system settle. She felt less bewildered. She was clearer about the task at hand. By the end of the session, Aliyah decided that she would allocate 30 minutes a day for the next two weeks to mapping out the skeleton of a strategy while making sure her teenage self was close by to jump in when needed. In the meantime, that teenager would be happily doing something else.

This visualization exercise sounded a bit out there to Aliyah. However, because she felt so much better in session, once the vision came up for her, she was game to try it on her own in the coming weeks.

In our next session, we barely started before she announced excitedly, "Rachel. I built the strategy! It worked! Visualizing giving my 13-year-old a break worked." Things had profoundly shifted because we involved Aliyah's survival mechanism, we didn't reject it. We appreciated it for what it had to offer. We kept it occupied while Aliyah did what she needed to do and allowed it back in for refining the strategy once it was built. We didn't say, "Get out of town, 13-year-old." Instead, we got curious about the thirteen-year-old's wisdom and got to the root of the problem.

Compassion toward ourselves starts to unravel the stuck places by allowing us to witness and acknowledge our inner world. Kindness toward those parts of ourselves that have been doing the heavy lifting beneath the surface of our awareness gives us the space to leverage the wisdom and let the rest go.

Let's be very clear here. Kindness to yourself, compassion for yourself, does not mean anything goes. It is not a free pass. It does not mean you can let yourself get away with indulging what isn't serving you.

It is *compassion with accountability*. In Aliyah's case, though her 13-year-old voice had a lot to offer, she was disrupting Aliyah's ability to successfully build the strategy for her team. Being compassionate does not mean being accommodating. It does not mean being a doormat.

Applying this same compassion to myself, my habitual response of criticism towards my husband when receiving generosity made sense. My extremely uncomfortable visceral response when attempting to not speak critically toward my husband signaled just how powerful and deeply embedded these beliefs around generosity were. With the pressure I felt to please a benefactor for our family's survival and the way I felt beholden to any kindness, I can and do feel deep compassion for the little girl who took all that on, unbidden. I can understand the pattern of rejecting or deflecting acts of kindness or generosity that emerged from my childhood.

The resulting behavior, however, was not ok. Continuing to criticize my husband when he was being kind was not going to support a successful relationship. If I wanted a loving, connected relationship with my husband, I needed to change my behavior. I needed to have both compassion for and accountability to myself. I needed to acknowledge where this behavior was coming from with reverence. And then, I needed to change my behavior.

Compassion means being able to say to your inner world, "What is going on is not okay. So let's figure it out together." It is vital that you be loving while you attend to what needs attending to. It is unhelpful to reject your survival mechanisms and resistance. It is also unhelpful to let them continue to run the show. Compassion doesn't mean burrowing under the covers and avoiding what's going on.

In every interaction, in every relationship, you bring in your old patterns; your resistance, and your survival mechanisms, everything we've discussed up to this point. Having compassion for yourself acknowledges that, in any interaction, you bring your history to the current moment. You bring your intergenerational history, home history, race, gender, cultural background, trauma, the list goes on. You bring all of this into the room always, and especially when you lead.

Compassion for yourself requires that you be kind to your survival mechanisms. It takes time to cultivate this compassion. We all can be so hard on ourselves. You must honor the information your survival mechanisms hold because their wisdom allows you to show up better as a leader. You need to be clear on what that wisdom is so that you can hold yourself accountable in shifting the behaviors that are no longer helpful. Practicing compassion with yourself is just that: a practice. Ordinarily, our go-to is to be hard on ourselves, so we need to learn a new way of relating to our resistance and survival mechanisms.

Take a moment and give it a try. Identify a pattern, survival mechanism, or resistance that's keeping you stuck—perhaps one of the ones you identified in a previous exercise.

Then, disrupt it. Ask a "what if" question. If you're stuck making a decision, you could ask, "What if I just say YES?"

Notice: what is your immediate internal response? Does an underlying belief come to the surface?

Challenge that belief: How true is it? Poke holes in its logic. Visualize the holder of this belief. What age is the holder of the belief? What are they wearing? Who do they remind you of? Once you have that visualization in mind, pause and acknowledge how that mechanism has helped you. Thank it. Identify the wisdom it is offering you. Don't rush this part. As I talked about in the chapter on understanding resistance, the more slowly that you go through this step, the faster and longer-lasting your results will be.

Finally, find a different job for your survival mechanism. Or, as in Aliyah's case, give it an opportunity to take a break. Allow it to go on a vacation. Find a way to work with your pattern, rather than rejecting it outright.

High performance as a leader requires that you change your definition of success. Your performance is directly related to your relationships with people: your direct reports, your cross-functional relationships, your leader. As we've peeled back the layers of your inner world in this book, you can see how for these relationships to work, you first have to know yourself.

This is why it's so vitally important for you to understand and disrupt your patterns, embrace your survival mechanisms, and understand your resistance. Once you identify a pattern that's not working for you it is only natural to want to replace it with a shiny, new habit. But there is no skipping the inner process.

Each of the steps we've covered thus far is necessary preparation for you to experience powerful change. The following chapter is about the next step in developing new ways of being: challenging the assumptions you didn't even realize were there.

CHAPTER 12

Challenging Assumptions

"But when you drop your assumptions all together, your soul stands naked in the open fields of possibility."
—*T.K. Coleman*, Freedom Without Permission

"Ilya has been with us forever… *I can't just ditch him.*"

Suni, co-founder and Chief Marketing Officer, and I had been working together for about a year when she came into our session with an employee dilemma. You first met her in the chapter on cultivating awareness.

Together, we had softened Suni's sharp elbows—so much so that Rebekah, her co-founder and best friend, had reached out to me privately. "Rachel, I don't know what you did," the email read, "but she is like a different person." Team members were no longer avoiding her, they sought her out! Now that Suni was showing up as a different leader, we had the opportunity to work on more subtle and sophisticated leadership skills.

"I hired Ilya less than a year after Rebekah and I started the company," Suni said during our session. "And about a month ago, I brought on a VP over him and his team. And Ilya was like, 'What if they fire me when they come in?'"

"'I won't let that happen,' I told him."

I could see where this was going.

"I promised him, Rachel! The thing is… Ilya is not in the right role. The company is so much bigger now, we really need someone with a different skill set in his position. It's part of why we hired the VP

115

over him in the first place. And, long story short, well, we can't find another role that works for him. I am a woman of my word," Suni concluded. "But now I don't know what to do with him."

Suni had over-promised and put herself in a difficult position as a leader because of her loyalty to her team members. It wasn't the first time this issue had come up. I suspected an "if/then" belief behind what was emerging as a pattern for Suni. As in, "If I hire someone and they demonstrate unfailing loyalty by sticking with us through the bumpy beginning, then I am obligated to..." What? The end of that statement was going to have to come from Suni, but my radar was up. When we make if/then statements, it's an indicator of a survival mechanism—which may be making assumptions about the current moment that aren't true.

I knew this behavior was a pattern for Suni because not two sessions before Suni had shared with me, "My director of marketing is struggling. I told her, we'll hire you an executive coach. And if you can step it up in the next three months, we'll promote you to VP."

My eyebrows had shot up. "Do you think three months is a realistic timeline?"

"The Board does not think this individual is at all capable of being a VP. And if I'm totally honest," Suni had said, spreading her hands, "No, I don't think she can turn it around in three months."

"And yet, you promised to invest in her and put extra energy into helping her to be successful."

"Yep. Exactly. She's been with us since the beginning."

Fast forward to the current session. It was important for Suni to reevaluate her beliefs around loyalty. We now had two different situations where she had over-promised underperformers and put herself in a difficult position. The employees that Suni felt such loyalty to, whom she had hired so early in the company's existence, were still not performing and were failing to meet her expectations.

"I'm curious about the message you're communicating to employees and how that aligns with what you actually want to be communicating," I said.

"I've been their cheerleader. I'm trying to get them to the next level." Suni said. She had come a long way from her sharp elbows communication style. However, she now seemed to be over-indexing in the opposite direction.

"Yes, you have been their cheerleader. But you have not been clear about your expectations of them. And this is now creating difficult situations for everyone. Let's get to the heart of where this is coming from," I said.

"I just need to have a conversation with my employees, with each of them," Suni said.

"'*I just need to...*' is a great indicator of resistance," I reminded her. "The 'just' indicates that it hasn't happened yet... So, what is getting in the way?"

Suni looked at me wordlessly, eyes wide.

"Uncovering the resistance is important to truly shift the behavior," I said. "Since resistance is an indicator of a survival mechanism, and the survival mechanism is a belief system that needs to be updated...Maybe we need to reevaluate your definition of being loyal," I suggested.

"They've been with me from the beginning when we didn't know if we would get enough funding to pay them. They took a chance on us. I feel like we need to take a chance on them."

"You may be making some assumptions here that we have to challenge. Being loyal doesn't need to mean you owe someone something. Being loyal can mean having someone's back, setting someone up for success, prioritizing transparency in your communication, and caring about them as a person," I said.

Challenging assumptions is the next pillar in the MettaWorks method. It is where we go beyond habits and patterns to shifting belief systems. Suni's belief system here was that the definition of loyalty to her employees is owing them a job even when they can no longer deliver.

How do you know when an assumption is in place and possibly in the way? Some verbal red flags of unhelpful assumptions include, as I mentioned, if/then ("If I do X, then Y will happen") or either/or statements ("I can have this, or I can have that, but I can't have both"). These statements contain an implicit assumption, a preconceived idea that is creating boundaries around a decision. One of the ways to engage with an assumption or limiting belief is to consider, "What if that isn't the case?"

"It's important for you to be able to speak candidly about what you need from these employees and how they are delivering on that—or not," I said.

"I can't do that! I'd be abandoning the team members who've been with us the longest," Suni protested.

"Okay, let's examine the truth of that statement," I asked. "You can be loyal and appreciate all that Ilya has contributed up until now. And you can acknowledge that this role is no longer a good fit for him. Both can be true. You can communicate this message clearly and kindly. You have the skills already! You've done so much work around how you talk to your people."

Suni looked crestfallen but nodded.

"The problem is, what you're thinking of as being their 'cheerleader' may actually be limiting their growth, as well as the company's growth. Alternatively, saying 'I see you, we value you,' and then setting clear expectations about their role and responsibilities is to the benefit of all," I explained. "It's a both/and. What would that look like? How would that feel?"

"Hard… and a relief," Suni admitted. "If I'm honest with Ilya about what's expected of him, he can either deliver or pursue something that is more aligned with what he does bring to the table. He was great when we were a scrappy little start-up…"

"So… not abandoning him?" I recalled Suni's earlier words.

"No, I guess not," Suni said with a wry smile. "Now that we're bigger, on a different trajectory… Ilya might actually enjoy working in a smaller company again. It could be an opportunity for him."

Often, assumptions have a lot to do with identifying what is within and what is beyond our control.

A few sessions later, Suni announced, "I did it."

"I went to Ilya and spoke honestly with him," she said with a sigh of relief. "I told him that our expectations of his role were changing. And that we hadn't been seeing the performance we wanted to see to meet those expectations. I also apologized and said that it was on me. It was on me for not communicating that clearly, or sooner."

"We met a few times, actually," Suni continued. "After a few conversations around the expectations, how Ilya could grow to meet them… He came back to me and said, he appreciated my transparency, and that it was time for him to find a new role. Ilya decided ours wasn't the company for him anymore."

Later still, Suni shared that Ilya had landed in a new role at a smaller company where he gets to do what he is best at. Suni letting go of her assumptions around loyalty and doing what made sense for the business was a gift to Ilya and herself.

Unexamined assumptions can create problems throughout our life. When my first son was born and I returned to work, I allowed myself to switch between only two states: working or taking care of my son. There was no in-between; that was the only way to be a good mother and a good professional. Those two states didn't include rest or restoration time for me. I had no life outside of work and my child. It was not healthy, not to mention completely unsustainable.

Something had to give. As I examined the story underneath this untenable situation, I realized that my definition of a good mother (any moment not spent working needed to be spent mothering) was not true. I'm allowed to have adult conversations; I'm allowed to eat out. I cultivated a new habit that allowed space for these things.

After my second child was born, I fell back into some of those old patterns and old assumptions without even realizing it. Unbidden, I would take both sons longer at night, tending the newborn whenever he woke, so my husband could sleep through the night. His paternity leave ended before my maternity leave was over, so I felt it was more important for him to get sleep before going off to work. I prioritized this belief over the rest I needed. I disregarded my own needs and instead attended to my 3-and-a-half-year-old, breastfed and took care of my infant son, and all while recovering from a Cesarean. It was, to put it mildly, hard and stressful. I was exhausted, depleted, and sleep-deprived.

I was taking care of everyone else first and doing it all myself. The thing is, I had done a lot of work to prioritize my health with my first son. Now, challenged with these new circumstances (a second child), old assumptions and beliefs that led me to deprioritize my own health and well-being, began rearing their unwanted heads again, influencing how I showed up as a mother of (now) two.

Shocker: I developed a heart arrhythmia. We're not talking about, oh, an occasional skipped beat. I literally didn't feel my normal heartbeat most days. Six weeks later was Thanksgiving. By then, everyone knew about my heart arrhythmia. My mother, father, and brother were there; my husband's mother and her partner were there. My husband, relegated to the kitchen for six hours as he cooked a beautiful meal, was unavailable to help with the kids. My health was compromised, I was mother to a 6-week-old and a three-and-a-half year-old, and was still recovering from a cesarean section, a major surgery and now had a severe heart arrhythmia. And yet, I tried to be a hostess. I took full responsibility for the kids.

Ironically, the five fully-grown adults who outnumbered my two small children could have easily, and happily, taken over for a few hours. I could have spent the whole day in bed, and let them help. I had a perfect justification and multiple reasons to hand over the reins. Instead, I pushed myself to attend to my children the whole day. I made assumptions about what I needed to do for everyone else to make them feel cared for.

As a result, another shocker: my arrhythmia worsened.

After the end of a long day of taking care of everyone else, it became crystal clear that the heart arrhythmia acted up when I said yes to something that I wasn't actually okay with. Thanksgiving put a spotlight on the fact that the arrhythmia worsened when I attended to other people's needs without them even asking me to do so. It had to do with my own assumptions about others' needs. Pattern identified. Totally unconsciously, I was putting everyone's needs ahead of my own, to my own detriment.

Once a pattern is identified, the next step in the MettaWorks method is to disrupt the pattern. The moment my heartbeat started skipping, it was a signal to pull back and create boundaries. The thought of disrupting the pattern of attending to everyone else's needs created a lot of anxiety for me. Whose needs are not being met right now? Am I being selfish? Am I causing harm?

Now, if I were to take myself through the MettaWorks method, it was time to embrace my survival mechanism. It wasn't my first time dealing with this particular mechanism; the belief that if I take up space for myself, it will cause harm to others. Here I was again, attending to my perceived needs of others, whether asked or not.

Okay, I've been here before. And so yes: I've done this, I know this, and it still took me all of those steps to get to here. It took a heart arrhythmia to get me to notice, "Oh, right. This is an (old) pattern of mine." As I've talked about before: it's a spiral journey. And although I was revisiting an old belief, because of the amount of personal work I have done, the process happened faster, and I recognized it more quickly than I ever had before.

What fueled the situation with my family, and caused me to fall into some of my old habits, were assumptions I was making that I needed to challenge. These assumptions defined what my responsibility was when the family was at the house for Thanksgiving.

My assumption was that I needed to take care of the kids because I was the mom. Therefore, it was my responsibility. On Thanksgiving, I made assumptions about everyone else and what they could or should handle. The question I could have asked myself at the time was: what is my responsibility at Thanksgiving? What did I actually need to be in charge of, given my circumstances; recovering from a c-section, having a 6-week-old infant, and a legitimate medical issue?

This process applies to all aspects of your life, professional and personal. I am constantly challenging the assumptions of my leaders, talking to them about their true responsibility and role. Here's your chance to challenge your own assumptions:

Consider a seemingly untenable, impossible situation at work, especially in your relationships.

What are the statements you're making about the situation? Are there any if/then, either/or, or other absolute statements in place?

Ask yourself:

To what degree are these statements true?

If true: What do I need to do to make them *not* true?

What would having both/and look like?

When you begin to challenge your assumptions, it allows you to shift your unhelpful belief systems, so that you can create new habits to replace them. Shifting your belief systems enables you to work with your colleagues and teams, unfettered by unconscious bonds to old stories, experiences and triggers, that have no place at work.

Without doing the subterranean work of challenging the underlying assumptions, often, those new habits can't be established. My experience isn't unique, as you'll see in the next chapter. Shifting those belief systems is what allows you to create new habits to replace the old patterns, sustainably and for good.

CHAPTER 13

Nurturing New Habits

"Forget inspiration. Habit is more dependable. Habit will sustain you whether you're inspired or not."
—Octavia Butler

"Ugh. I did it again, Rachel."

Chris is the founder of a successful 50-person start-up and a MettaWorks client. Concerned about a client escalation, he had recently reached out to an individual contributor no less than four layers of management down from him. He was disappointed in himself and brought it to our coaching session to discuss and debrief.

For the prior few months, Chris and I had been working on helping him trust and empower his people, taking himself out of the day-to-day. Previous to our work together, Chris' involvement on the ground had created a great deal of chaos as well as a huge bottleneck on many decisions. He had made a great deal of progress around this behavior, which is why he was frustrated with his own behavior in this particular situation.

"I've done so much work on this… I feel like I'm regressing!" Chris heaved a sigh. "I thought I fixed this already. Why am I doing this again?"

"When you're changing a behavior that has been a habit, it's not one and done," I said.

"Well, it's frustrating," Chris huffed.

"It's actually a good sign," I countered. "Often our expectation is that now that we have committed to a new behavior, the old one will just go away. It doesn't work like that. Let's step back for a moment. How did you know you'd slipped up again?"

"That was the feedback I got... The IC mentioned it to their manager, and before I knew it, the VP of Product was slacking me about it."

"Hold on. We need to celebrate for a moment!" I said to Chris. He shot me a sidelong glance. "Are you being sarcastic?"

"Ha. No. I'm serious! This is the first time you got direct feedback. That is because of the work you've done to pull out of the weeds and increase your approachability. The fact that you got feedback at all is a milestone. So what did you say to the VP?"

"Well, he was like, 'Dude, that wasn't cool,' and I was like, 'Oh my God, you're absolutely right!' I immediately apologized to him." Chris nodded, reflecting. "In retrospect, I realized it was inappropriate to reach out to someone four layers beneath me. I just got so worried about the client issue, I wanted an immediate answer...! I can see how I was coming from a place of reactivity."

"I'm impressed, Chris," I said. "You've come so far. You recognized that you made a mistake. Tell me, what exactly did you take away from this situation?"

"I get how I completely undermined all those layers of management and created mass panic among their people," he said. "I don't think I would have seen that a few months ago before we started working together. I really wanted to make it right this time. I've already circled back to all parties involved and apologized via email. And I requested that if this happens again, they should push back and send me to their manager."

"Any thoughts on how to help prevent it from happening again?" I asked.

"I'm way ahead of you, Rachel," Chris teased. "I told my direct reports, 'I need you guys to help me deal with my frustration of not knowing what's going on. I need you to send me a weekly update on the project.'"

"Chris! This is great. Well done! That's the deal with nurturing new habits: you will screw up. It's a given. Recognizing this is an opportunity to recommit to the habit. That is exactly what you did, step by step: acknowledging that you made a mistake, identifying what set you off course, and putting systems in place to prevent it from happening again."

When we nurture a new habit, it opens up a whole world of possibilities. We had no idea what was possible before. We were unaware.

As many of my clients have put it when talking about how powerful coaching with MettaWorks has been for them: "Nothing has changed, but everything has changed." Even within the same organization, with the same peers and stakeholders, our experience of the company changes when we nurture and bring new habits to fruition. This is the power of new habits.

You can't get to the new habits unless you identify your drivers and cultivate awareness. You cannot begin shifting into new habits until you challenge the assumptions driving the old habits.

Once you create a habit, life doesn't change immediately. For better or for worse, this is not an on/off switch or a one-and-done kind of deal. The reality is that you have trained yourself in your old habits for most of your life. Once you create a new habit, you need to keep doing it over and over again. You need to keep recontracting. You need to keep recommitting.

Often circumstances will show up to test you on your commitment to your new habits. Circumstances will sow seeds of doubt in your new habits. Your job as a leader is to recommit again and again.

When you notice that you are sliding back into old habits, that's the moment to acknowledge that this is a good sign! It can feel like you are sliding backwards, or "regressing," but it's the opposite. Noticing that you are slipping into old ways indicates that you are paying attention. You have become aware of the old habit you are recreating, and you want to do it differently. That is terrific! You then have the opportunity to recommit to your new habit and strengthen your relationship with it. In that moment of recognizing your old habit, it is important to remember the new habit you have created, why you created it, and how it feels to continue to employ it.

Just like with resistance, when it shows up again and again, "breaking" a new habit or struggling to stick with it is a good sign. So, ok, you stumbled. You also noticed and responded to the misstep. You can now approach it differently. Compassionate accountability plays a role here, as always. Don't kick yourself. Be kind to yourself, and recommit to the new habit. (By now, you can see more clearly how the pillars of this process are not linear; they loop back on each other, overlap, and interconnect.)

My heart arrhythmia that arose after the birth of my second son provided an opportunity for me to recommit to a new habit (and be compassionate with myself). As I mentioned in the previous chapter, the habits I'd cultivated with my first child seemed to go out the window with my second.

The arrhythmia and its repercussions only got worse after Thanksgiving. When I started not being able to breathe well, things got really scary. I fell apart emotionally. It was time to nurture some new habits. This was only possible because I had started challenging the recurring assumptions that led the old habits to resurface in the first place. Something needed to change. I now needed to recommit to prioritizing my health. The new habit I had worked so hard to cultivate with my first son as an infant now needed to be nurtured and strengthened.

Just like my clients, I couldn't skip any steps. The driver was easy to identify; my health was seriously not okay. Turning things around was the only option. I made an appointment to see a cardiologist.

"Oh, I'm not worried about this," the cardiologist said, cheerfully. "You just need to lower your stress and get more sleep."

"Uh, thank you? And, how exactly am I supposed to do that..?"

He just looked at me and said, "Why don't you do a hypnosis session with me. We can see if it makes a difference. If it calms you down, it'll help indicate that this is stress."

I blinked. Of course I get the only cardiologist I've ever met who's schooled in hypnosis. I'll chalk that up to good karma. "Okay, I'm on board," I agreed.

During the ten minute hypnosis session, my nervous system was able to relax in a way it hadn't in months. Not surprisingly, my heart kept a normal heart beat throughout the session.

After hypnosis, I walked away wondering, "Which stress exactly do I need to attend to?" Stress is such a large bucket. Was it the anxieties around being a mother of two? Was it worrying about my company while I'm on maternity leave? Could it be the complete and total lack of sleep? I reached out to my mother, who consulted her network. She came back to me with a solution for my sleep deprivation: "You need to get a night nurse."

A what? I didn't know this kind of person existed. It turns out that if you pay an exorbitant amount of money, you can afford to have a lovely human being, specifically trained and exceptionally skilled, take care of your newborn baby. The woman we hired would sit with our youngest son all night and only bring him to me when he needed to feed. I could finally get a few hours of uninterrupted sleep.

At first, hiring a night nurse was a difficult decision. All my resistance reared up. Remember, resistance protects our deepest fears. Here, my fear was of being a neglectful mother. In the end, we decided to hire a night nurse because my health was on the line.

This is the journey of nurturing a new habit, a new way of being. It requires us to remind ourselves why we want the change in the first place. I wanted to be able to take care of my family but also take care of myself. I wanted to be healthy and happy and have a healthy and happy family at the same time. My new habit was meeting others' needs and also meeting my own.

When difficulties cropped up, as of course they did, I could have gone to the place of "I'm a terrible mother, I abandoned my infant son and put him in the arms of a stranger at night." Instead, I reminded myself, "It was vital to my own well-being and my ability to be a good mother; I needed to get the night nurse. I'm trying to figure out my stuff, I'm trying to disrupt old unhelpful patterns." And by the way, the night nurse taking care of my infant son was kind, responsible, deeply caring, and highly experienced. My son thrived as a result of her care, and I started to thrive once I recommitted to my new habit of taking care of myself as well.

I consider this an example of how far I've come. I've built so much more capacity. The opportunity to recommit to a habit I'd started forming with my first child when I had my second meant that I was ready to shift my survival mechanism of attending to others' needs over my own. It is powerful and vital for me to equally honor my sons' needs and my own in the face of feelings of guilt, unease, and anxiety. This is the work of nurturing a new habit!

I want to acknowledge here that your mindset, after you create a new habit, is still fragile. You are not entirely convinced that the new habits you've created will be effective. The first challenge you encounter after creating your new habit can be destabilizing. In the face of a challenge to the new habit, it can be easy to say, "Well, that didn't work," or "I can't do this." This is where consistency is imperative. Data collection on how the new habit is working is important to strengthen your trust and resolve. Nurturing a new habit is a special, even sacred process. New habits are like little seedlings; they're very delicate, and deserving of a lot of care and attention.

This is also where the skill you've cultivated, compassionate accountability, comes in. Remember, a misstep or regression is to be celebrated. Be kind and firm with yourself, recommit. You are ready to deepen the habit. It's a spiral journey. Don't stop. Keep going.

Now it's time for you to apply this in your own work.

First step: Notice when you think you're "regressing" or stumbling when establishing a new habit. Reframe this awareness as a positive. It means that you have an opportunity to recommit to the new behavior or habit—which is the whole point. It means you're doing it right.

Next: notice what theme is at play when you're having trouble with a new habit. Notice what is happening when you break the habit. What circumstances or feelings come up in the moments before you "regress"? Is there a feeling of urgency or anxiety?

Each decision is a series of micro-decisions. Where could you have paused? Where was there an opportunity to decide differently, leading you not to break the habit?

Finally: How can you recommit to your new habit right now, in the moment? What supports can you put into place, such as Chris did, to help you stay on track?

Change isn't always rainbows and unicorns. Change is messy, and involves missteps and apologies. Missteps and apologies strengthen your success as a leader. People are watching you lead with sincerity. They see your interest in changing. Nurturing new habits, and recommitting to them when you stumble, makes you a better leader.

You may be thinking, "That sounds great, Rachel, and it sounds hard." (No lie, it is.) So, how do you keep going, even when you're challenged to establish and nurture a new habit that requires you to recommit, and recommit, and recommit yet again? Re-introducing your north star and the next pillar of this process: your ideal state. You are ready to dream bigger than simply your anchor in the storm. You are ready to take the drivers you identified at the start of this spiral journey to a new level.

CHAPTER 14

Ideal State

"It's not: you'll be happy when you're a good leader. It's actually: to be a good leader, you have to be happy."
—Rachel Rider

"I never imagined it could be like this," Jonas' eyes were wide in amazement. "I'm not getting up in the middle of the night... I have a great team in place...And now, I get to ask for—*more??* I find myself thinking about: where is my time best spent?" Jonas said.

Jonas had originally come to me because he was stuck in the weeds and had gotten feedback that he was micromanaging. He had since come a long way from waking in the middle of the night to attend to a problematic server (as you may remember from the chapter on pattern identification). When you're in the weeds, it's impossible to think bigger. You simply don't have the necessary perspective to look at the big picture. When you have the time and space to think about your ideal state, you have already come a long way as a leader.

This mindset shift in Jonas was a big deal. When Jonas first came to me three years ago, he just wanted to stop the bleeding. Now, he was considering what he wanted his ideal work situation to be. Jonas was a perfect example of a leader poised and ready to think about his ideal state. He was thinking about the ideal way to invest his time and energy. He was dreaming about the impact he could have beyond his company.

This is what imagining the ideal state means: your why beyond the drivers you may have identified at the start of this journey. While your drivers are your anchors through the storms along the way, your ideal state is the best version of the manifestation of your anchors.

For example, Yetunde's anchor, her original driver as we learned in the chapter on identifying drivers, was about making resources available to underprivileged people through access to coding skills. Once she had gone through the pillars of this process she had time and space to reflect on her ideal state. She became aware that she wanted to make an impact on a much larger scale. She wanted to level the playing field for everyone entering the tech industry regardless of their background or education at the national level and even inform and influence policy.

The ideal state is the magnification of the things that are important to you. Going through this work, you move from being stuck in the weeds, putting out fires, or immobilized by unhelpful patterns, to greater freedom and wider spaciousness in your time and energy. This affords you a broader perspective. Having done the inner work, you now have the capacity to dream bigger.

Jonas was able to start investigating his ideal state because of all the work he had been doing with his coach up until that point. For Jonas, as we met and worked through each challenge and opportunity that came his way, the value of having a neutral sounding board and advisor was proven, time and time again.

With results as positive as they were, Jonas continued to work with a coach for three years, and his career continued to flourish and quickly evolve. To be clear, you don't need three years to get to your ideal state. Jonas' career trajectory was accelerated, so there was a great deal of time spent on triaging situations and engaging with different leaders. When (and only when) Jonas reached a place of stability in his career did he have the space to look around and consider what his ideal state looked like.

During our first year working together, our focus was on helping Jonas to shift his mindset around: "What does it mean to lead?

How do I get out of the doing?" Our sessions were about relationships and facilitating conversations.

Not long after the server incident, he stepped into a difficult role. He inherited a very toxic team and an organization that undermined him at every step. Direct reports would disagree with the direction Jonas gave and go straight to Jonas' manager to complain. They would consistently commiserate among themselves to create strategies that would undermine decisions Jonas made.

Not only did he have to increase productivity, he also had to gain the hearts and minds of his team. This was no small feat. The organization lacked a larger vision and systems to support that vision. Through our work together, Jonas was able to articulate a vision of the organization that inspired his people. He empowered his team to build and implement processes and systems that further drove investment in his larger vision.

About a year and a half in, as Jonas honed his skills as a leader, he got promoted to a much larger role. He had completely turned the organization around. (Hence the promotion). That same formerly "toxic" team ended up throwing him a party. In an act of celebration of and reflection of their deep affection for Jonas, they bought him all of his favorite libations, updating the labels with his likeness and most well-known sayings.

Fast forward to the current session; he had been firmly ensconced in his new role for about a year. Jonas continued to mull over his ideal state, "I don't want to waste energy on places that aren't meaningful to me, you know? I've been thinking about that, and... well, my legacy."

I nodded encouragingly. "This. Is. It," I said. "This is the indicator that you're at the top of the mountain, Jonas. You have cleared it all, gotten out of the weeds. You now have the time and space to look at these things. This is the point at which you step into a new level of leadership. You're looking at the view, and you're saying, 'Okay, what is my ideal state? Who do I want to be? How do I want to create time for myself? What do I want my life to look like?' This is the fruit of all of the work that you've done, and that we've done together."

Sometimes you can't imagine how things can be different until you're on the other side of the overwhelm. You can't imagine what good could look like until you are no longer in a state of overwhelm of juggling so many things at once.

When you are at this stage of the MettaWorks method, you've gone through the process of identifying your drivers. You've worked on cultivating awareness so that you could identify your patterns and see what happens when you disrupt them. You've started to embrace your survival mechanisms and understand your resistance. You've turned your survival mechanisms into your superpowers, through cultivating compassionate accountability. You challenged your assumptions, creating the space for you to nurture new habits.

Through this process, you got to a place where you have delegated effectively, driven alignment with your team and peers, and have successful partnerships across the organization. Although the work is ongoing and there is always room to go deeper, things have changed. You now have time to ask yourself: "What do I do now with so much more time on my hands? What is my role supposed to be now? Now what?"

This is the point at which I ask my clients: "What would you love to do? What would you love your role to be if you could have anything you wanted? How would you love to spend your time if you could spend it any way you wanted?"

Clarifying your ideal state and articulating what you truly want for yourself is a powerful action that moves you from scarcity to abundance.

The expansiveness of the shift is profound. Besides the fact that you've gone through this process, pulled out of the weeds, and now have time during the day, dependent on your current environment not much else has to change in terms of your external circumstances, at least the circumstances beyond your control. You can still work with the same people, at the same company as when you started this journey—but your experience of it has utterly transformed.

Your focus is no longer on "not enough": "There's not enough time. There are not enough resources. I don't have the right team." Your new focus now embraces possibility: "How do I want to spend my time? How do we leverage our resources productively? How do I partner effectively? How do I use my team successfully?"

Your approach and perspective have shifted irreversibly. It is a mindset shift and change of experience in the very day-to-day fabric of your work and life. Your world opens up.

This practice of identifying your ideal state is the result of your evolution from reactivity to becoming proactive, as Jonas exemplified. Your drivers, the ones we first identified and defined in that topic's chapter, may be the same but they look different from this perspective.

In the beginning, when you identify your drivers, there are many constraints that come up. "Yeah, but... I can't... If I don't do this, I won't be able to, etc." After doing this work, going through the MettaWorks method, you have the opportunity to walk out of the dense forest of tasks into this beautiful green field of open space. You now get to ask, "Oh, what do I want to do with this time I have, with this space in my calendar?"

For me, I knew I'd reached this stage in my own work and company recently. I had pulled myself out of the weeds and I was celebrating my success at doing so. It was year-end planning and during a coaching session at that time my business coach asked me, "Okay, so now let's dream about what you want next year to look like and feel like. Let's talk about your ideal state for next year."

My reply surprised me a little. "I want more time and space to think about the direction of my company. I want more time to be with my children. I want my days to feel spacious and relaxing. I'm going to try for a 20-to-25-hour work week, while increasing my income."

This may not seem all that remarkable. However, for me, historically, I worked 50-to-60-hour weeks. My days were filled with clients; I accepted everyone my impossible schedule would allow. It used to be that I couldn't find enough time in the day for as many clients as possible and the internal meetings to run my company. To consider going to a third of the hours while maintaining the same revenue was a huge deal. My mindset was now, "That's what I'm going to do" instead of "That's impossible, what about...," or "There's no way I could..." The internalized objections and naysayers were now gone.

Not only were the inner limiting beliefs gone, I accomplished what I set out to do! I hired a team of highly qualified coaches trained in the MettaWorks method and put a cap on how many clients I would personally see, at an increased rate. My working hours decreased. I had more thinking time to be strategic about my company. I wrote this book. I spent more time with my children.

More important than how I did it, was the fact that I could consider it at all. I pulled out of the weeds enough to be able to dream about my ideal state. That was the true indicator of the transformation that had taken place. You can only accomplish a goal once that goal is well articulated and clear. Once upon a time, I couldn't have even imagined that increasing my revenue while reducing my working hours was an option. It wouldn't even occur to me that this was something I could desire, much less achieve.

To be frank: It takes a lot of work to get here. And: it's worth it. It is life-changing to have spaciousness in my day. I now have the ability to set company goals based on my internal compass, without inner judgments, objections, and old stories. This doesn't mean the drivers aren't the same. In fact, my drivers simply solidified and became clearer to me: more time with my kids, more spacious days, more doing the kind of work I love. These were not new drivers.

The heart of your drivers might not change, but they will look different at this stage of the process. They are magnified. Your openness to the possibility of achieving and expressing your drivers and your confidence in manifesting them have expanded. When the distractions fall away, there is room to actually create your ideal state, there is so much more space to dream. So much more is possible.

As Jonas defined his ideal state and thought about his legacy, his priorities shifted. The things that used to bother him, like the interpersonal politics surrounding his role, or the toxic parts of the company, didn't bother him anymore. Rather, these items may still bother him but they no longer monopolized his time and energy as they used to. These things became less of a distraction for him because his focus had changed. What he previously let sap his energy was simply a minor distraction or a part of the day's usual work.

The legacy he was going to leave, and what his name was going to represent inside and outside the organization—these became Jonas' focus and north star. Like Tara's mantra for her, Jonas' ideal state had a clarifying effect, slicing through the minutiae to uplevel his focus, and uplevel himself. He was better able to prioritize, and quickly focus on what mattered most. He started empowering his people at a whole new level. Even for me, my challenges felt less like obstacles because I had a clearer vision of where I was heading.

Defining your ideal state makes you a better leader. This is only possible at this stage of the game, after you've done the inner work. It increases your impact, as Jonas' story demonstrates. With your ideal state as your north star, and the skills you've developed going through these pillars, distractions fall away and your priorities become crystal clear. Your ideal state makes you more effective. It allows you to be more decisive in how you direct strategy and people.

Your ideal state, besides being tied to your success as a leader, is also connected to your happiness—even beyond your success. I cannot tell you how many leaders I've worked with who will testify to this: It is not necessarily the case that you'll be happy when you become a great leader. Reaching the goal does not deliver happiness.

Instead, it's actually that to be a good leader, you have to be happy. Articulating your ideal state and using it as your north star ultimately fulfills you and brings you joy in your work. It is not the role itself, no matter how good you are at it. These emotions are contagious, and will spread to your team and organization, further advancing your effectiveness in leading them. By pursuing what is possible, by embodying this profound mindset shift as a leader and embracing your ideal state, you impact your people. They, too, can now see what is possible. They will follow your inspired leadership as a result.

So how do you begin envisioning your ideal state? I like to go back to *Sesame Street*. *Sesame Street* has a mantra they repeat during every episode, where whenever the characters encounter a problem, the solution starts with:

"I wonder... What if... Let's try..."

Ask yourself some of the questions Jonas asked himself:

Where is my time best spent?

Who do I want to be?

What do I want my life to look like? What do I want my legacy to be?

Begin your responses to these questions with: I wonder, what if, let's try...

I've said it before, and I'll say it again: High performance as a leader requires that you change your definition of success being measured by the amount of work you do. In actuality, the less work you do, the more successful you are. Additionally, the same skills that make you successful—bonus!—also make your work easier, make your life happier, and you, more fulfilled.

To be fulfilled in your life, you must feel fulfilled in your work. Anything less means feeling stagnant and stuck, alienated from all you could become. When life and work align, those same work hours become a creative expression of what's uniquely yours; the perspective, insight, and skills you and only you bring to the table.

Articulating your ideal state makes it possible to execute your vision. This is where you get to really decide who you want to be as a leader. In this next chapter I want to share with you a part of my journey and who I want to be as a leader.

CHAPTER 15

Liberation: What Frees Me as a Leader

"The master's tools will never dismantle the master's house."
—Audre Lorde

I had followed my own advice. I had done the inner work, still ongoing and yet sufficient to have created a beautiful life for myself, aligned with my ideal state. I felt satisfied and spacious. If not stress-free, then stress "light." I could genuinely say that I was happy.

It was around this time that I was attending an event at the Buddhist community of which I had been a part for a very long time. My place of refuge, this community, had been a place to reflect and explore my inner world since I was a girl. I felt deep gratitude for how far I'd come from my experience as that thirteen-year-old, anxiously carrying my family's survival on my shoulders. My inner work, including my meditation practice, had taken me to such a happier place in my life. Over the next two hours however, I had an experience that would launch me on a profound journey, taking me to my next level as a coach, leader, and human.

For the first time in the history of my Buddhist community, a panel made up of community members of color was held, to discuss their experience within the predominantly white space. It was painful for me to listen to them talk about how unwelcome they felt. These were the voices of people to whom I felt deeply connected. These were the voices of people I'd known for decades. I sat next to these folks for weeks in silent meditation. And they were saying that not only did they feel unwelcome, they often felt invisible or singled out.

I felt like the rug had been pulled out from under me. To hear that my "safe place" caused harm to others felt disorienting and confusing. It totally destabilized me. This was my first awakening: racism exists everywhere, including in a community of good white people. Racism exists here, even here, where we are deeply committed to cultivating awareness, compassion, and relieving the suffering of all sentient beings. Despite loving intentions, the centering of white culture was happening (and continues to happen) without my awareness. The door cracked open on a perspective I'd never recognized before. It made me curious. If this was happening here, what was I doing every day that perpetuated the discomfort of those around me?

This shift, and what I've been learning since, have disrupted deeply-held assumptions entirely invisible to me up until that moment. As a result, it feels vital for me to include this chapter as a continuation of my journey as it is deeply connected to the MettaWorks method. Anti-racism work has given me the opportunity to inquire: Who am I as a leader? Who do I really want to be? Antiracism work is what has helped me unravel unhelpful belief systems within myself and thus, support that deep work within my clients. Antiracism work is what has given me permission to be more of myself and challenge internalized unhelpful cultural norms and expectations. I write this chapter not as an expert, most certainly not as an antiracism coach, but as an ongoing learner bringing her experience as an offering to her clients.

After my profound experience with my Buddhist community and then the confluence of the pandemic and George Floyd's murder, I decided to hire an anti-racism coach Makeda Pennycooke, who I still work with to this day. I hired Makeda because I was feeling ill equipped to support my clients of color in using the right language. I was worried about my company composition and the lack of diversity on the team.

The truth is, I was approaching anti-racism in the very way I discourage my clients from approaching leadership challenges: I thought anti-racism was a superficial issue. Thus, I treated it as such. I thought I just needed to use the right language and hire the right-looking team. Though these behaviors are incredibly important, they are less than the bare minimum required.

This is often what leaders think when they encounter roadblocks at the highest executive levels. There is often a lack of understanding that struggles at this level are much more complex and sophisticated than a superficial change of behavior. Doing anti-racism work is the same. The more you dig in, the clearer it is just how deep the layers of conditioning and racism go.

Through my work with Makeda, I came to realize that my anti-racism journey was less about tactics, as I'd once supposed, and more about me looking at my whiteness and how I perpetuate white culture.[6] For example, it has been humbling to notice, much less admit, that I've coached my clients of color differently, often without even noticing. I came to realize that, more often than with my white clients, I tell my clients of color what to do. Despite my extensive training and experience, I would subtly move into telling mode more than coaching mode with my clients of color. I made this precise misstep one day and brought it to a session with Makeda.

"Ugh, I really stepped in it, Makeda. Again! I keep perpetuating white standards... Like I'm the expert in the room. Instead of acting as a true partner to my clients of color. It happened again today with Kendra."

I sighed. "Maybe I'm not the right coach for her."

Makeda looked at me pointedly, a hint of a smile playing around her lips. (She, too, is compassionate and also very good at holding me accountable.) "So, what you're saying, Rachel, is that you should start refusing to work with leaders of color? Because you made a mistake?"

---

[6] The Elements of the White Middle Class Dominant Culture were first identified by Kenneth Johnson and Tema Okun in 1999. To learn more about these characteristics visit: https://www.whitesupremacyculture.info/characteristics.html

I grimaced. "I see your point."

"This client has been working with you for over a year," Makeda continued gently. "She's clearly receiving value from the relationship."

"That's true," I said. "I just feel bad that I continue to screw up in this way. Frankly, I feel ashamed."

Shame can be a huge roadblock to doing deep anti-racism work, something I continue to learn over and over again. I often find myself immobilized by the shame of what I've done in perpetuating harm as a white person.

"Shame is a way for you to lie to yourself," Makeda replied matter-of-factly. "And, unless you've committed a truly terrible act, the shame is usually lying to you . So when it arises, particularly in anti-racism work, it's critical to see it as a lie. If you continue to believe it, it paralyzes you instead of allowing you to learn and move forward."

"I can see how people would just shut down. I literally just did it," I admitted.

"You will mess up. It's inevitable," Makeda reminded me. "It's a predictable part of this process. What's vital is that you stay in it. That you don't give up. That you acknowledge what went wrong and work to do better. Just like you did with your client."

"Let's pause for a moment, to celebrate that," she continued. "You, making mistakes, rectifying them, and committing not to do them again—that IS anti-racism. You're doing it; you're doing the work. Remember, Rachel, anti-racism work is sowing seeds for future generations. You may not see the fruit of your labor in this lifetime. But that doesn't mean you should stop."

In the past, when I felt shame around my actions as a white person, I would find myself becoming defensive. This may sound like the familiar dynamic of being in resistance so as not to acknowledge the underlying fear—because it is. "But I'm a good person! I didn't mean to do that. I didn't realize. I didn't know," I'd protest internally.

Until I recognized and understood it as resistance, it was hard for me to closely examine my behavior. I let the shame keep me stuck in the good/bad binary of: either I am a good person who is not racist or a bad person who is racist. As I've been learning, this binary is not only false, it could give me a way out of the work altogether: if I tell myself, "Hey, I'm a good person. I can't be racist. This doesn't apply to me," then I give myself an out to bypass the work and keep perpetuating the culture of whiteness and causing harm.

Doing the inner work changes you from the inside out, getting to the root causes of your challenges for sustainable, long-lasting change. Anti-racism work is no different. I came to learn that I don't need to be overtly prejudiced or racist with a capital "R" to unintentionally perpetuate systems that cause harm to people of color. There is so much more going on that I create without intention, particularly around race, which is vital for me to be aware of as a white leader. Examining my own implicit racism has required that I go through the same pillars of the MettaWorks method outlined in these pages, on an even deeper level. I am striving to dismantle harmful beliefs and behaviors I've taken as truth my entire life. I use the present tense because this is an ongoing process for me.

This new perspective allows me to bring a different lens when coaching my clients. There is more space for me to be curious about the veracity and benefit of cultural norms in the workplace. There is more space for me to hold space with my client to allow them to explore who they are within these norms, which norms do they want to choose to participate in, which norms do they want to challenge.

Antiracism work demands that I look deeply at the subtle, sophisticated patterning that I have absorbed as a white person. As inner work, it is not one and done. I need to be vigilant: looking at patterns, challenging my assumptions, catching missteps, and working to correct them through nurturing new habits every day. Persistence and consistency are important here.

Anti-racism work has allowed me a timely, critical opportunity to apply everything I have learned thus far. My own inner work up to this point can be a template for disrupting my racism and internalized sense of superiority (tied to being white) that harms people of color. I want to be a leader and coach who creates a container of safety and respect for all people.

Anti-racism work has allowed me to challenge assumptions I've made implicitly about performance, perfectionism, and the "right" or "professional" way to do things. I've learned to question what it means to have a high standard of performance, to look at perfect vs. good, and consider the wisdom in constantly iterating rather than striving for an assumed single "perfect" endpoint. This awareness has helped me understand how the culture of whiteness is oppressive to white people too.

Nothing exists in a vacuum: this book, the MettaWorks method, your leadership, none of it. I take my own leadership development very seriously. I have taken myself through the MettaWorks method more times than I can count. Examining my cultural conditioning, particularly around whiteness, has become an incredibly important part of this process.

Just as survival mechanisms are the invisible driver behind the steering wheel of interpersonal interactions, social conditioning plays a similar role. Social conditioning may be even more insidious because the culture at large supports me in ignoring the assumptions, beliefs, and systems around whiteness that are shared across that culture. Put another way, this conditioning is the dominant narrative that influences everything from social status to the very ways that people do business, choose what to prioritize or value, and how to structure a company or team.

If, as a white leader or white passing leader, any part of you identifies with wanting to explore this work with curiosity, please do so. There must be some wanting that compels you down this path, because it's hard. It feels like a slog if it doesn't light your heart up. I showed up to anti-racism work with a hunger to be perceived better. Through this work, I went from wanting to be perceived better to fundamentally questioning beliefs I took as fact for my entire life.

My choice is what gives me freedom as a leader. I want to show up as I choose, not as I'm unconsciously driven. This is why this work has become so important to me, and inexorably shifted how I show up as a leader. Anti-racism work has made me a better version of myself, a better me. It invites me to access a part of myself I've never worked with before. As a leader, anti-racism work has unlocked possibility: what is possible when every person in my organization feels safe, unencumbered, and free to express and exchange ideas and energy, including me the leader? How much happier could people be in such an environment, myself included? What possibilities are unlocked in terms of aspiration, innovation, and performance?

Relationships are vital to my work as a coach, just as they are vital to any leader. At this level, my success and my client's success depends on the quality and strength of our relationship. In successful relationships, people feel seen. They feel heard. They feel safe. They feel that they can have candid conversations. When people feel safe they will actively trust and seek you out as a sounding board. You become the leader they look to for inspiration and guidance.

This is why I have chosen to, and continue to, do my own personal antiracism work as a white individual. I have consistently, explicitly and subtly, perpetuated white culture. I so often unintentionally hold white culture as the right way to do things. It is unhelpful to the work I do and the clients I serve. This deep patterning within me needs to change.

Confronting these issues demands a much more sophisticated lens on how I relate to people to develop fair and equitable relationships with everyone. This is why I include this chapter. I simply cannot cultivate the safe, trusting relationships with my clients and my team on which my success depends without actively looking at my white filters. If you are a white leader reading this, I invite you too, to examine your white filters.

Your success as a leader is about your relationships with your people. The only way you show up for your people is to show up for yourself. The more I do my inner work, the bigger the ripple effects are on my company, on my leadership, and on my success.

This is the realm of possibility.

CHAPTER 16

A New Realm of Possibility

"Your vision will become clear only when you look into your heart. Who looks outside, dreams. Who looks inside, awakens."
—Carl Jung

Imagine a life where your day flows with ease, confidence, and purpose. Imagine that you deeply trust your internal compass. Imagine that you show up as your true self throughout your day.

You are able to initiate an uncomfortable conversation without putting it off or perseverating over it. You delegate effectively. You show up to work with a calendar cleared of projects and meetings that don't require you. Instead of moving through your day in a reactive, heightened state, your day is spacious. You have choices about how you spend your time and energy.

People seek you out for your opinion. Your influence is felt and recognized by your people and beyond. You are considered an asset to the leadership team, your colleagues, and your industry. You work happier. You are fulfilled and satisfied with your results and impact.

All this is possible. All of this happens when we have a deeper understanding of ourselves and thus the people on our team, our peers, and other leaders.

It takes work. It takes a lot of work. The work can also be powerful. The work can be fun. You start to change your relationship with your inner world. You start to pay attention to the unspoken communication between you and another person. When you do this, when you integrate the pillars of the MettaWorks method into your day-to-day, your life can change.

When your interpersonal relationships change, your performance as a leader dramatically improves, and so too does your work experience. When you can trust your team to get things done, there is deeper ease in how you show up. You have a deeper confidence and understanding of yourself. You know how to show up effectively, without being caught flat-footed in any situation, whether in the room with important decision makers, or simply in a meeting with a difficult personality.

When you cultivate a better relationship with yourself and others, you experience profound ease. It starts with the way you run your team and company, leveraging the skills we've unpacked over the course of this book:

Identifying your drivers, even amid challenging situations. How can your actions move you forward if you can't define what you want and where you want to go?

Cultivating self-awareness by continually gathering data to understand what makes you and your people tick. There are always invisible, unconscious elements at work behind the scenes.

Reading the room by strengthening your internal compass, so you can interpret others' reactions with confidence, trusting the unspoken information you gather without needing explicit feedback.

Identifying the patterns that aren't working, that are impeding your progress. When you understand how you create or perpetuate these patterns, you can profoundly change how you show up and strengthen your relationship with others.

Disrupting these patterns, which often sparks a visceral, intense emotional response. That response reveals what is hidden underneath: the internal, unconscious survival mechanisms that have been in charge.

Embracing those survival mechanisms without ditching or contradicting them. Instead, celebrating these mechanisms that have protected and helped you for years. You now have the space to choose how you want to respond.

Understanding and allowing for resistance indicating that survival mechanisms have been embraced and are shifting, ready to be liberated. Rather than fighting the inevitable resistance that comes up, understanding and working with it.

Harnessing survival mechanisms for good. When you educate the survival mechanism and don't let it drive, it can become one of your great superpowers. It's not about surgically removing your issues but understanding how they serve you and putting them to good use.

All of this requires *cultivating compassionate accountability*. Compassion truly witnesses and acknowledges without judgment. Accountability says, "I hear you, and this isn't okay. So, what are we going to do about it?" Now you can act from a place of choice.

Challenging the assumptions your survival mechanisms make about the current moment. Remember, these beliefs aren't true. You can start to create new conversations and patterns without abandoning your convictions.

Nurturing new habits to replace harmful patterns is not a one-and-done. It is a continual process of recommitting and recommitting and recommitting.

Visioning the ideal state means you get to operate at a different level. From a perspective now aware of assumptions, mechanisms, and patterns, you expand your vision. You see the forest for the trees. It takes a great deal of work to get to this point. It is a huge accomplishment!

Incorporating anti-racism work to challenge culturally conditioned assumptions and belief systems. Unlock a deeper level of the trust, performance, and creativity of all of your people.

From this new expansive perspective, and only from this perspective, can truly new solutions and opportunities present themselves. Having moved through and past the reactivity, histories, and heightened emotions that were present at the earliest stages of this work, you have access to your authentic self. By knowing yourself better, you show up better interpersonally: by strengthening trust, communicating effectively, and lowering your reactivity, you become a better leader.

This book alone won't make you a better leader. It is next to impossible to effectively do this work on your own. If you truly want to implement this work, make sure you have your own board of directors or support system. I mentioned my own support system in the acknowledgments of this book; I have an army of healers and coaches and teachers. Yours can include experts who help you shift behaviors that no longer serve you and coaches who educate you on new ways of being. Your board can include friends and family who support you unconditionally. It can include peers who tell you not what you want to hear but what you need to hear. You're human; you learn lessons and forget them. Patterns resurface, and you revert to old behaviors. Everyone needs their own board of directors. Please consider this book as a step toward building your support team.

Dear reader, if you take nothing else from this book, let it be this: You have an inner world that exists, and that inner world is a treasure trove.

My wish for you is to understand that your inner world informs a lot of your behavior. The more you are aware of, understand, and intentionally harness your inner world, the more the world is what you want it to be. It is equally important to note that the more you remain unaware of your inner world, the more that inner world will make decisions for you without your input or control and will be the result of unintentional disappointment, pain and suffering. Cultivating relationships with your inner world provides so many gifts.

You can be wildly successful. A different experience of your life is possible; in these pages, I've shared the pillars and tools I use. The client stories reflect the power of this work, and the possibility of change. People's lives change through this work. I, myself, am a result of my own work.

Look at this beautiful life you have already created for yourself. Look at the success you have already achieved. You are already at this level in your career because of the trust your people already have in you.

Our happiness in our work and life creates a beautiful loop, a wheel of creation: one begets the other, in an ongoing, generative cycle. It is my humble wish that this book helps change your life.

If this book does even a part of what I wish for you, then the seed has been planted for transformation. As we reach the end of our time together, you are already at this beginning of change.

May your experience of life change, even if nothing outside of you changes.

May you wake in the morning happy and excited for the day, and may you put head to pillow at the end of the day feeling fulfilled and at peace.

May you become exactly who you want to be.